THE WARREN BUFFETT OF INDIA
Rakesh Jhunjhunwala

THE WARREN BUFFETT OF INDIA
Rakesh Jhunjhunwala

MAHESH DUTT SHARMA

PRABHAT
PRAKASHAN

Published by
PRABHAT PRAKASHAN PVT. LTD.
4/19 Asaf Ali Road,
New Delhi-110002 (INDIA)
e-mail: prabhatbooks@gmail.com

ISBN 978-93-5488-638-6
THE WARREN BUFFETT OF INDIA: RAKESH JHUNJHUNWALA
by Mahesh Dutt Sharma

Edition
2024

Price
₹ 350 (Rupees Three Hundred Fifty Only)

Printed at
Sita Fine Arts, Delhi

Author's Note

Rakesh Jhunjhunwala, an investor, and an Indian business magnate managed his portfolio as a partner in his wealth management firm 'Rare Enterprises.' Rakesh Jhunjhunwala was popularly known as the 'Warren Buffet of India' and the 'King of Bull Market.'

Born on July 5, 1960, Rakesh Jhunjhunwala's net worth was approximately $ 5.8 billion, which is 5,900 million US dollars. Rakesh Jhunjhunwala was married to Rekha Jhunjhunwala and the couple has three children.

Rakesh Jhunjhunwala grew up in a Rajasthani family in Mumbai. His father worked as a Commissioner of Income Tax. Within the family, he was known as 'Rakesh' and his ancestors were residents of Jhunjhunu in Rajasthan. Rakesh graduated from Sydenham College and thereafter enrolled himself in the Institute of Chartered Accountants of India (ICAI).

In December 2021, Rakesh Jhunjhunwala started his own airline company 'Akasa Airlines.' Former CEO of Jet Airways, Vinay Dube is the CEO of Akasa Airlines.

Rakesh Jhunjhunwala was the chairman of Hungama Digital Media Entertainment Pvt. Ltd. and Aptech Limited. He was also on the Board of Directors of 'Geojit Financial Services', 'Praj Industries Limited', 'Provogue India Limited', 'Bilcare Limited', 'Concord Biotech Limited', 'Prime Focus Limited', 'Innovassynth Technologies (India) Limited', 'Mid-Day Multimedia Limited', 'Nagarjuna Construction Company Limited', 'Viceroy Hotels Limited' and 'Tops Security Limited'.

Rakesh Jhunjhunwala's biggest investment in 2021 was Rs. 7,294.8 crores in the Titan Company. Also, he held stakes in privately held companies such as Metro Brands Limited, Concord Biotech Limited and Star Health Insurance. Moreover, Rakesh Jhunjhunwala was a member of the Advisory Board of India's International Movement to Unite Nations, also known as the Indian International Model United Nations (IIMUN).

The readers can consider this book as a bible for stock investors — a unique, readable, and collectible book.

Contents

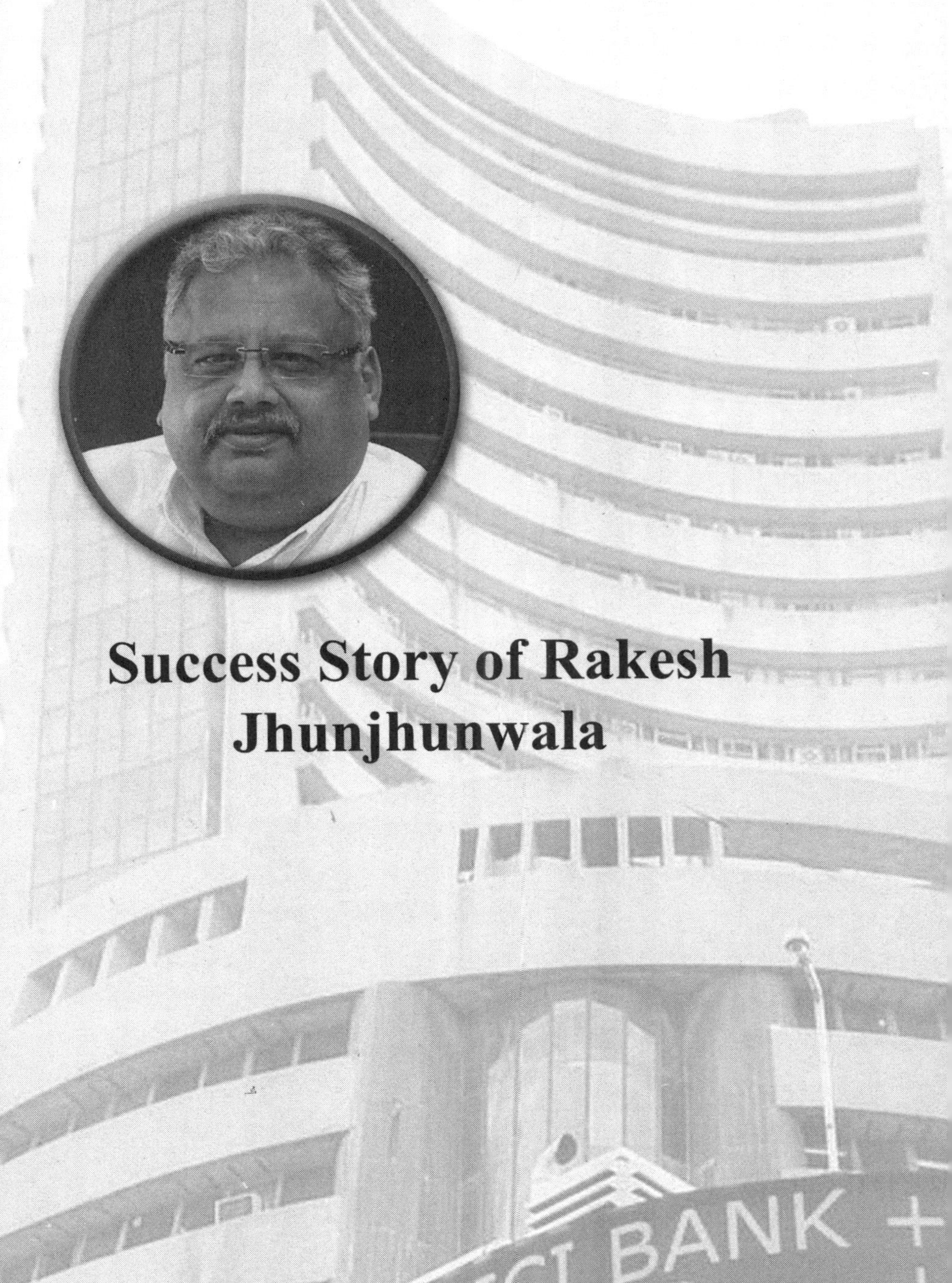

Success Story of Rakesh Jhunjhunwala

There are very few investors in the Indian stock market, who started with just a few thousand rupees, but today they have become one of the most affluent people in India. Their speciality is that the shares of the companies in which they invest money, see outstanding earnings. Hence, if common investors also invest in such companies, they can also earn better profits. You too can benefit by following the strategies of such people. One such person was 'Rakesh Jhunjhunwala', who was called the 'Warren Buffet of India'.

Rakesh Jhunjhunwala was an investor and share trader of India. He was a Chartered Accountant by profession, and his company was 'Rare Enterprises.' He was known as a prominent investor. He started with an investment of Rs. 1,200 in 1985. The first stock he bought was of the 'Tata Tea.' In 1986, he earned a profit of Rs. 5 lakhs by selling those shares. Before his demise, his net worth was Rs. 44,300 crores through his business of share investments. He was the 36th richest person in India.

Famously known as the "Big Bull" and "India's Warren Buffet", it was said of Rakesh Jhunjhunwala that whichever share he invested in, it was likely to appreciate.

Investors consider his tips to be the best, but hardly anyone knows who was his 'guru' (teacher) in the stock market. Rakesh Jhunjhunwala affirmed that he reached the heights of success because of the teachings of his guru.

As per Rakesh, his father taught him life values and helped him in taking momentous decisions. His father believed that one should not hesitate while taking major decisions.

According to him, he got support from multiple people in his life, but above everyone else, he believed in his father. He considered his father as his first guru or teacher.

As per Rakesh, his father taught him life values and helped him in taking momentous decisions. His father believed that one should not hesitate while taking major decisions. Other than his father, his other teachers were Radhakishan Damani and Ramesh Damani. They also guided him on multiple occasions. Radhakishan Damani is also counted amongst the select rich people of India and is a billionaire investor and businessman. He owns the retail chain known as D-Mart. As per the Bloomberg Billionaires Index, he is the world's 98th richest person and the 3rd richest person in India with a net worth of $ 11.2 billion.

Ramesh Damani is a member of the BSE (Bombay Stock Exchange). Other than this, he is also known as a successful investor. Ramesh Damani has been working in the share markets since 1989. You will be surprised to know that when Ramesh Damani stepped into the share market, the Sensex stood only at 800 points. Compared to 1989, it has now increased by almost 55-60 times. Ramesh Damani is also known as the 'Nawab of Dalal Street.'

There is one more name on the list of Rakesh Jhunjhunwala's teachers. That person is Kamal Kabra who is also a stock investor. There was one more friend of Rakesh Jhunjhunwala (on the list of his teachers) who breathe his last at a relatively young age. His name was Rajiv Shah. Jhunjhunwala used to say that they used to think of doing the right things. "We were bent on getting successful, but we never thought that it was going to be easy."

Jhunjhunwala used to say that they used to think of doing the right things. "We were bent on getting successful, but we never thought that it was going to be easy.

Mantra of Success

According to Rakesh Jhunjhunwala, his net worth was Rs. 1 crore in the year 1988, which increased to Rs. 200 crores in 1993. He said that it did not mean that at this pace his net worth reached Rs. 800 crores in the year 2000, but in 2002 also his wealth remained at only Rs. 250 crores. According to him, he invested almost 5 per cent of his portfolio in debt instruments. In accordance, between September 2001 and September 2003, he invested 40 per cent of his portfolio in debt instruments.

Jhunjhunwala completed his early studies in Mumbai and received his bachelor's degree from Sydenham College, Mumbai. He was also a film producer and the chairman of Aptech and Hungama Digital Media Entertainment.

> ***Rakesh Jhunjhunwala completed his early studies in Mumbai and received his bachelor's degree from Sydenham College, Mumbai. He was also a film producer and the chairman of Aptech and Hungama Digital Media Entertainment.***

Share investor, Rakesh Jhunjhunwala, earned seven times of his investment by investing money in a Sridevi film. Rakesh Jhunjhunwala and some other investors had invested Rs. 11 crores in the film and the film did a business of around Rs. 78 crores.

Rakesh Jhunjhunwala, who was generally known to invest his money in stocks, had invested in Sridevi's film *English Vinglish*. They made huge profits in the first week itself. You will be surprised to know that the box office earning of the film that was made on a budget of only Rs. 11 crores was Rs. 78 crores, i.e., the film gave more than 7 times the return on its investment. In this 133-minute film, industrialists like R.K. Damani and Sunil Lulla also invested their money and the film was directed by Gauri Shinde.

Let us inform you that apart from *English Vinglish*, Rakesh Jhunjhunwala had also invested money in *Ki and Ka* in the year 2016 and *Shamitabh* in 2015. The budget of *Ki and Ka* was Rs. 20 crores and it earned Rs. 100 crores at the box office.

Rakesh Jhunjhunwala invested in about 30 stocks and the value of his investment was around Rs. 15,000 to Rs. 16,000 crores. He made only marginal investments in the financial sector.

Rakesh Jhunjhunwala invested in about 30 stocks and the value of his investment was around Rs. 15,000 to Rs. 16,000 crores. He made only marginal investments in the financial sector.

Rakesh Jhunjhunwala held a 3.08 per cent stake in Federal Bank and the value of his stake was Rs. 320 crores. Till date, it had got a negative return of 40 per cent, while it gave a return of 52 per cent in one year.

Rakesh Jhunjhunwala held a 3.92 per cent stake in MCX. The value of his stake was Rs. 260 crores. Till date, it had got a return of 11 per cent, while in one year it gave a return of 51 per cent.

In NCC, Rakesh Jhunjhunwala held a 10.22 per cent stake and the value of his stake was Rs. 190 crores. Till date, it had got a negative return of 45 per cent, while it gave a return of 68 per cent in one year.

Rakesh Jhunjhunwala held a 5.53 per cent stake in Titan Company and the value of his stake was Rs. 4,900 crores. Till date, it had got a negative return of 15 per cent, while it gave a return of 25 per cent in one year.

> ***Rakesh said, "I have also learnt a lot because of my mistakes. Always learn from mistakes in life. An investor should always be like a chameleon. He should believe in himself and stick to that investment by making the right investment at the appropriate time."***

Rakesh Jhunjhunwala held a 7.42 per cent stake in Escorts and the value of his stake was Rs. 955 crores. Till date, it had got a return of 65 per cent, while in one year it gave a return of 82 per cent.

Rakesh Jhunjhunwala held a 5.49 per cent stake in CRISIL and the value of his stake was Rs. 670 crores. Till date, it had got a negative return of 11 per cent, while it gave a return of 18 per cent in one year.

Rakesh Jhunjhunwala held a 1.51 per cent stake in Lupin and the value of his stake is Rs. 615 crores. Till date, it has given a return of 18 per cent, while in one year it has given a return of 20 per cent.

Rakesh Jhunjhunwala held a 4.41 per cent stake in Jubilant Life Sciences and the value of his stake was Rs. 475 crores. Till date, it had got a return of 25 per cent, while it gave a return of 36 per cent in one year.

Rakesh said that you can learn everything from your mistakes. He said, "I have also learnt a lot because of my mistakes. Always learn from mistakes in life. An investor should always be like a chameleon. He should believe in himself and stick to that investment by making the right investment at the appropriate time."

❑

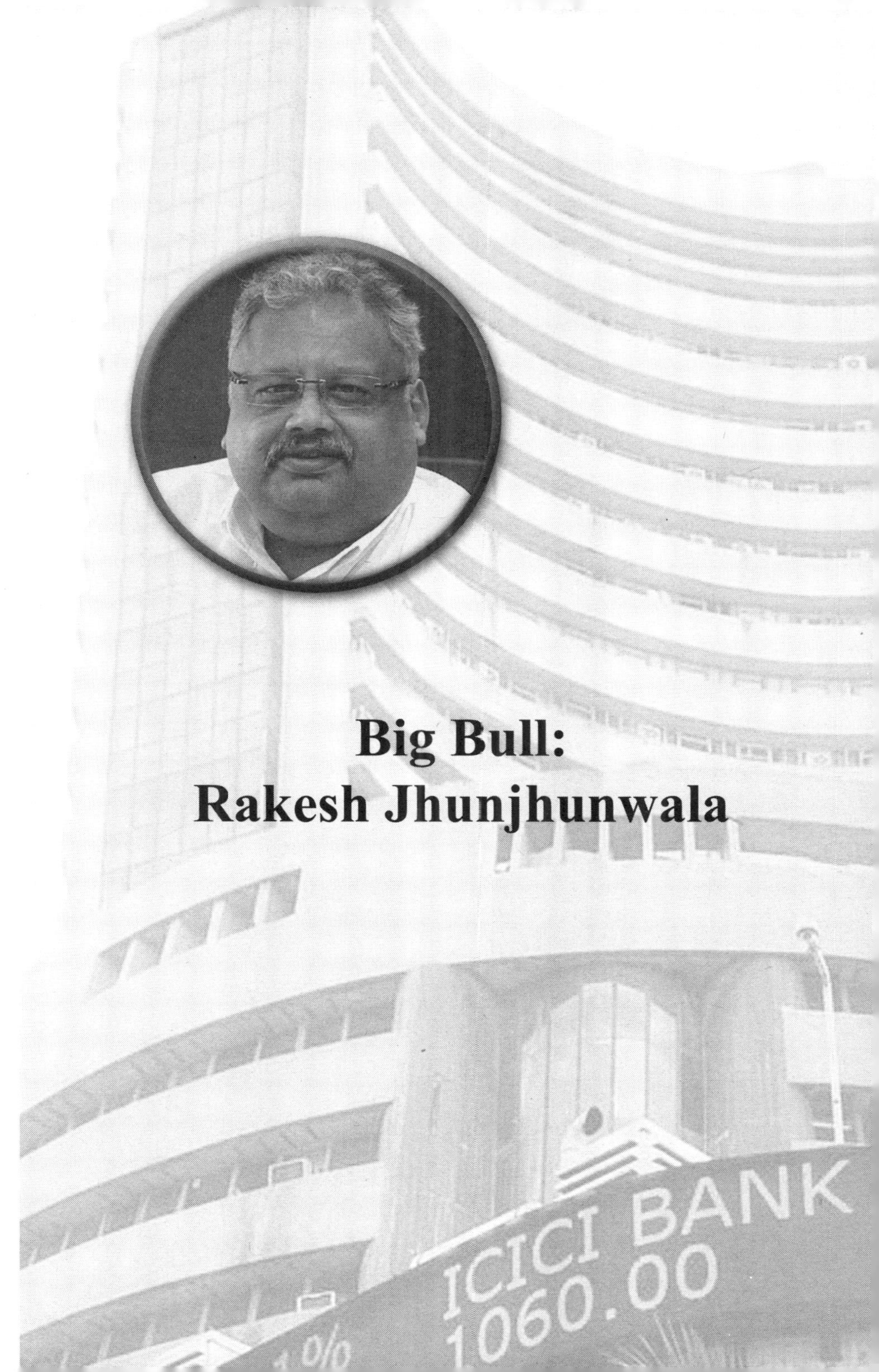

Big Bull:
Rakesh Jhunjhunwala

Rakesh Jhunjhunwala was called the 'Shahenshah of the stock market.' Some refer to this veteran stock market investor as the 'Big Bull,' while others refer to him as the 'Warren Buffet of India.' A comparable example of value creation that Rakesh Jhunjhunwala has set cannot be found easily. This is why even great investors would wait for his decisions. They wanted to know which company he planned to invest in and which would he be exiting from. Everyone would wait for the Big Bull's earning mantra.

Rakesh Jhunjhunwala was known as the 'Warren Buffet of India' due to his ability to make profits from investing in stocks. He was one of the richest private investors in the country. According to Bloomberg estimates, Jhunjhunwala had shares worth Rs. 11,140 crore. He bought shares in Aptech for the first time in the year 2005 at a value of Rs. 56 and his family members now hold 49 per cent stake in Aptech. According to the closing price of Aptech's shares on BSE, the value of the shares of Jhunjhunwala and Family is approximately Rs. 690 crores. The management control of Aptech was with Jhunjhunwala. Aptech is a company associated with education. Rakesh Jhunjhunwala was previously its chairman.

Rakesh Jhunjhunwala's portfolio was heavily focused on consumption-oriented stocks. He had invested in around 30 stocks. The value of his investment was around Rs. 15,000 to 16,000 crores. He made marginal or minimal investments in the financial sector.

Rakesh Jhunjhunwala was known as the 'Warren Buffet of India' due to his ability to make profits from investing in stocks. He was one of the richest private investors in the country.

Rakesh Jhunjhunwala held a 5.53 per cent stake in Titan Company and the value of his stake was Rs. 4,900 crores. Till date, it has got a negative return of 15 per cent, while it has given a return of 25 per cent in one year.

Rakesh Jhunjhunwala held a 7.42 per cent stake in Escorts And the value of his stake was Rs. 955 crores. Till date, it has given a return of 65 per cent, while in one year it has given a return of 82 per cent.

Rakesh Jhunjhunwala held a 5.49 per cent stake in CRISIL and the value of his stake was Rs 670 crores. Till date, it has got a negative return of 11 per cent, while it has given a return of 18 per cent in one year.

Rakesh Jhunjhunwala held a 1.51 per cent stake in Lupine and the value of his stake was Rs. 615 crores. Till date, it has given a return of 18 per cent, while in one year it has given a return of 20 per cent.

Rakesh Jhunjhunwala held a 4.41 per cent stake in Jubilant Life Sciences and the value of his stake was Rs. 475 crores. Till date, it has given a return of 25 per cent, while it has given a return of 36 per cent in one year.

Rakesh's portfolio was heavily focused on consumption-oriented stocks. He had invested in around 30 stocks. The value of his investment was around Rs. 15,000 to 16,000 crores.

Rakesh Jhunjhunwala held a 3.08 per cent stake in Federal Bank and the value of his stake was Rs. 320 crores. Till date, it has got a negative return of 40 per cent, while it has given a return of 52 per cent in one year.

Rakesh Jhunjhunwala held a 3.92 per cent stake in the company M.CX and the value of his stake was Rs. 260 crores. Till date, it has given a return of 11 per cent, while in one year it has given a return of 51 per cent.

Rakesh Jhunjhunwala held a 10.22 per cent stake in the company NCC and the value of his stake was Rs. 190 crores. Till date, it has got a negative return of 45 per cent, while it has given a return of 68 per cent in one year.

Rakesh Jhunjhunwala's approach had always been to invest in the long term. He was still bullish about the Indian stock market, even in the time of the Covid epidemic. Rakesh Jhunjhunwala said that due to Covid-19, the growth rate of the country's economy may remain negative this year, but the weakness in the economy will not have much impact on the stock market. Jhunjhunwala, who had always been bullish on the market, said that he too was frustrated with the current market situation; but at the same time, he feels that the recent rally in the market may be the beginning of a new high. He believed, "the recent rally in the market could prove to be the beginning of a new bull-run in the market. The recent reforms made by the government in the agriculture and mining sector will have a positive effect, although the government needs to take additional or some more steps on the reform front. Also, RBI should do a one-time restructuring of the debt of companies."

Rakesh Jhunjhunwala said that due to Covid-19, the growth rate of the country's economy may remain negative this year, but the weakness in the economy will not have much impact on the stock market.

As per Rakesh Jhunjhunwala, small investments can lead to a big fund; but you get returns only when you invest money in the share market with the correct strategy and correct approach. India's prolific investor and market's big bull, i.e., Rakesh Jhunjhunwala, had made money out of money in the last two decades. He had earned crores from the market. He often shared his tips with his followers. People can earn from the share market by following these tips.

His perspective had always been about long-term investment. His usual advice to early-stage investors was to invest long-term. He believed that instead of earning profit in the short run, it is better to let the investment multiply over time. He believed that money should be given sufficient time to mature in the market. We may have to wait but we can be assured of the returns.

As per Rakesh Jhunjhunwala, small investments can lead to a big fund; but you get returns only when you invest money in the share market with the correct strategy and correct approach.

Rakesh Jhunjhunwala said that investment decision in a company is not determined by the share price of the company. Instead, the value of the company is more important. Often people prefer shares with higher prices, but it is important to see the company's performance over the last one to five years. If the company's outlook is bright and favourable, it will give you good returns despite the ups and downs of the market.

Rakesh said that investing in the stock market is not always as safe as in banks. There is a bigger return in the market but so is the risk as well. That is why it is important for us to invest money only after gathering complete information about the company. One should not invest money in a stock just because others are investing in it; it is probable that others can bear losses, but we may not have that ability.

Rakesh Jhunjhunwala said going forward, strong growth is expected in pharmaceuticals stocks. Apart from this, he was also positive about the banking and financial sector.

It is not necessary that a company which is performing well in the stock market will give you lucrative returns. That is why it is important to do a background check of the company before investing and see the dividend issued by the company. Dividend plays an important role in the stock market. If a company pays regular dividends for a long time, then it means that it is not short of cash. Companies with cash surpluses often do well.

You may have surplus money to invest, but it is not necessary that you invest all of it at once. There is nothing wrong with a desire to make a profit, but the (share market) rule says that only a small investment guarantees better returns. While investing money in any one stock, divide your investment amount into small parts and keep buying periodically. If the stock goes down, keep buying. This will reduce the average price of your purchases.

In the stock market, it is important to observe the level of debt in the company one is planning to invest. If the debt is less, then there will be no pressure for cash on the companies. But if the debt is high, the valuation of the company may fluctuate at any time. Hence, make sure to review the company's debt before investing.

Rakesh Jhunjhunwala said going forward, strong growth is expected in pharmaceuticals stocks. Apart from this, he was also positive about the banking and financial sector. He observed that the earnings of the banking sector are not expected to decline as much as they are predicted to decline. The valuation of banking stocks is positive currently. One can invest in bank shares at the current price. Strong growth is expected in this sector going forward.

Rakesh Jhunjhunwala was born on July 5, 1960, in Mumbai. His father was an income tax officer. Since he was very interested in the stock market, his father used to talk about stocks with his friends.

Rakesh Jhunjhunwala was born on July 5, 1960, in Mumbai. His father was an income tax officer. Since he was very interested in the stock market, his father used to talk about stocks with his friends. Rakesh listened to all these conversations since childhood. One day Rakesh asked his father why the prices fluctuate in the stock market. Then his father asked him to read the newspapers. This was his first lesson about the stock market.

Rakesh said that you can learn everything from your mistakes. He said that "I also got to learn a lot because of my mistakes. Always learn from mistakes in life. An investor should always be like a chameleon. He should believe in himself and stick to that investment by making the right investment at the opportune time."

❑

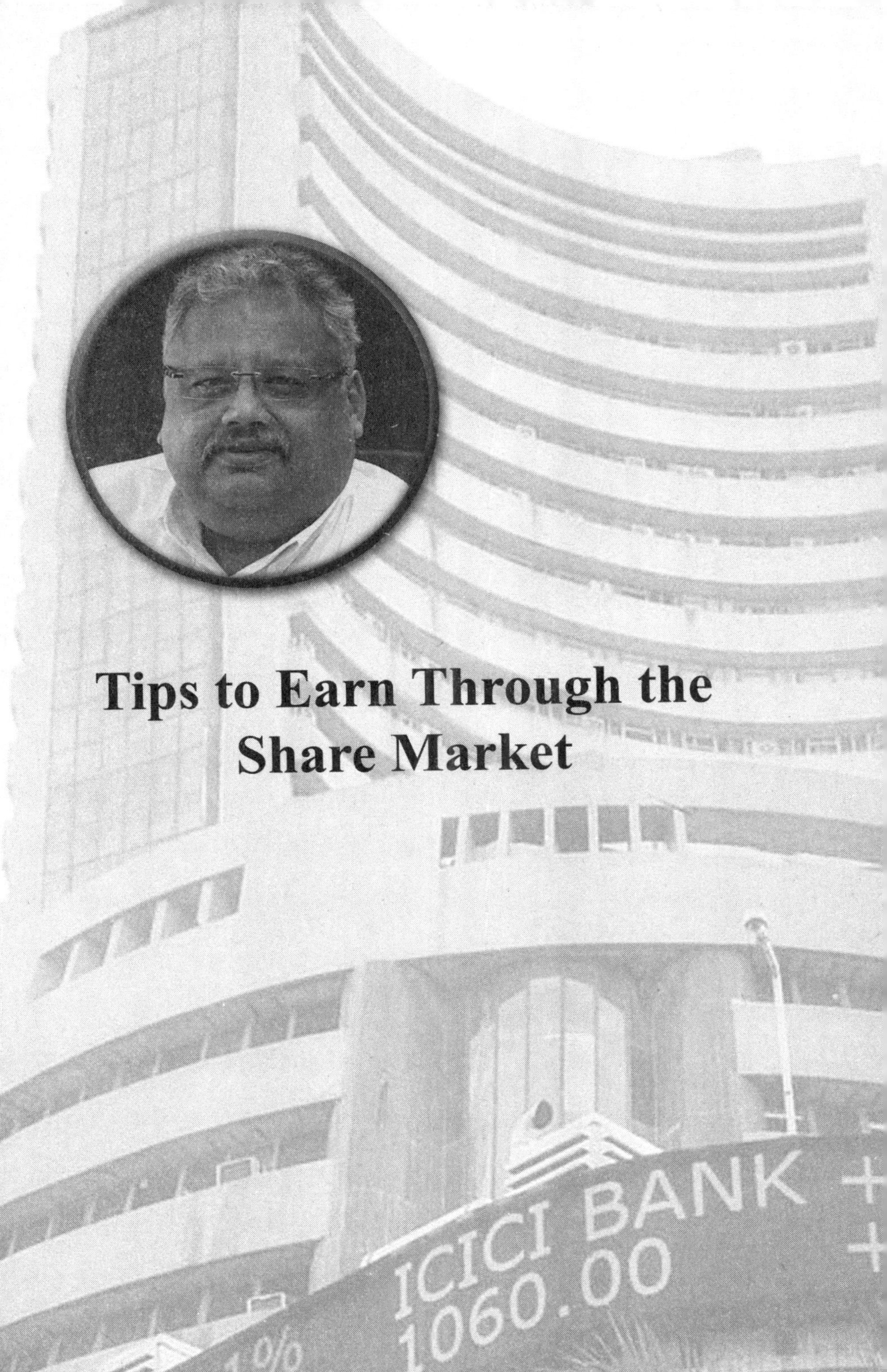

Tips to Earn Through the Share Market

Rakesh Jhunjhunwala has a special place in the investment world. He graduated in 1985 and started trading in the stock market full-time. At the time, only 150 companies were listed in the Sensex. Jhunjhunwala, who started with a mere Rs. 5000, had earned billions of rupees through stocks. He believed that passion is the key to make worthwhile investments; but along with passion, it is also important to have prudence. Jhunjhunwala was known as the 'Warren Buffet of India'. He was one of the richest investors in the country. He said this about investing in stocks, "Trading needs momentum. It is on the lines of take fast and give fast, kill, and run. Everyone wants to make money from trading, but it is not possible. I have lost money too."

Jhunjhunwala, who had witnessed all kinds of fluctuations in the market, did short selling from 40 to 100 in 1992. He believed that the biggest mantra to make money in the market is the bullish attitude. Most of the gains in the market come from maintaining the bullish trend. You don't necessarily have to be investment savvy, but you should have that temperament coupled with initiative and enterprise. Jhunjhunwala believed that investors should not forget their roots and should not pretend to be someone they are not. They should keep themselves simple. He warned that one makes the biggest mistakes in the best of times.

Jhunjhunwala said that if one has made up one's mind to earn money, then it is not necessary to start with a sizeable amount. One can become rich by starting small. All you must do is follow some basic rules of the stock market. These are the same rules that big investors have been following and today their names are included in some of the richest people. If you also want to earn well from the stock market, then you must pay attention to some important money *mantras* or golden tips, which can convert your small amounts into lakhs or crores, in a short time.

Rakesh Jhunjhunwala has a special place in the investment world. He graduated in 1985 and started trading in the stock market full-time.

It is said that the shares of whichever company that he spots, grow very well. One of his favourite shares is Escorts Tractor, which earned him a lot of money through his investments (in the company). Jhunjhunwala earned Rs. 284 crores in just 6 years by investing in Escorts tractors. In the September quarter of 2013, Jhunjhunwala bought around 5 million shares of Escorts tractors for the first time. Since then, it was one of his preferred stocks. As of December 2015, the number of Escort shares he held in his portfolio had increased to 11.2 million. He held about 9 per cent stake in the company. He eventually sold 1.2 million shares of the company in the December quarter of year 2017. Later he held 10 million shares and the shareholding in the company was close to 8.16 per cent. Escorts Tractor share price in September 2013 was Rs. 80. At that time Rakesh Jhunjhunwala had about 5 million shares, which meant that the total value of the shares was Rs. 400 million then. The current price of the stock as of the recent closing week was at Rs. 648. In this manner, the total value of those 5 million shares has now increased to Rs. 3240 million, i.e., a profit of Rs. 2840 million. If we consider the profit till date, it has been more than Rs. 2900 millions.

Jhunjhunwala said that if one has made up one's mind to earn money, then it is not necessary to start with a sizeable amount. One can become rich by starting small.

Rakesh Jhunjhunwala had invested heavily in many companies. A few companies owned by him gave him manifold returns during 2017. One such name was that of 'Geojit Financial Services', in which Rakesh Jhunjhunwala had bought about 7.6 per cent stake. The stock of this company increased by 245 per cent during 2017. Along with this, he also held 9.1 per cent stake in Escorts, which saw a rise of 118 per cent in recent years. Apart from these, Titan gained 90 per cent and the Autoline industry grew by 75 per cent. Jhunjhunwala had bought a significant stake in both these companies.

Don't Wait for the Right Time

Any time is the right time to invest in the market. Don't wait for the right time in the market. If the stock of a reputable company is at a reasonable price, then start investing, even if there is pressure in the market at that time. The common investor keeps waiting for the right time and is not able to invest in the market. Eventually, the investor, based on the market movements, invests in the stocks that have reached high levels and takes a loss.

Rakesh Jhunjhunwala had invested heavily in many companies. A few companies owned by him gave him manifold returns during 2017.

Don't Invest Based on Others' Investments

If you invest money in a stock just because others are investing in it, then you can incur a loss. The mantra to be successful in the stock market is not to follow people, but to make people follow you. Be alert when others are being tempted. At the same time, when others try to adopt a cautious approach, then start thinking about earning.

Don't Look at the Price, Look at the Value

Before investing, never think that just because a share is more costly, it will be better. Sometimes a stock priced between Rs. 50 and Rs. 100 may be worth more if the company is performing well. Before investing money in any stock, check the performance of that company. If the performance of the company is acceptable, then there will be no problem with the market's volatility.

If the stock of a reputable company is at a reasonable price, then start investing, even if there is pressure in the market at that time.

Trust the Companies that Give a Dividend

Before investing, check which companies are paying regular dividends. If a company pays a dividend on a regular basis, then it means that there is no shortage of cash with that company. Companies with cash surplus are also better performers. In such a situation, there is a chance of your money growing faster with the shares of these companies.

Choose Companies Which Have a Lower Debt

Before investing, also check which company has lower debt. On account of lower debts, companies don't feel pressurised for cash. TCS and Infosys are examples of such companies.

Don't Invest all your Money at Once

Stocks go through frequent ups and downs. In such a scenario, the thumb rule to make profits is to not make the entire investment at one go. If you want to invest in a stock, then divide the total amount into several portions and buy slowly. If the stock declines, then you should continue to buy and thereby reduce the average of purchases. So, strategize first and then invest.

Stocks go through frequent ups and downs. In such a scenario, the thumb rule to make profits is to not make the entire investment at one go.

Be More Practical with Regards to your Goals

There is no shortage of such stocks in the market, which have given more than 100 per cent return in a year. Strong stocks tend to see steady gains. Therefore, the probability to achieve high returns in a short period of time through stocks which are considered safe investments, is fairly low. However, such stocks can give you excellent returns in a longer run.

Don't Pay Attention to Rumours

According to Warren Buffett, checking stock prices repeatedly after investing in stocks is a wrong strategy. One should not do this for some time. The stock market is filled with rumours, so it is important to avoid them. Don't fall into the temptation of high returns. If you can visualise 15 to 20 per cent returns, then you should invest.

Buy the Right Stock and Hold on to It

Rakesh Jhunjhunwala said that it is impossible that everyone makes a profit during the boom time, and everyone makes a loss during a slump. He said that my business mantra is simple — 'Buy Right and Hold Tight', which implies that one should buy the right stock at the right time and then hold on to it.

Rakesh Jhunjhunwala said that it is impossible that everyone makes a profit during the boom time, and everyone makes a loss during a slump.

Invest in a Business, Not in a Company

The focus should be on the business of the company, rather than the company itself. An investor should always keep an eye on the kind of business the company is in, and how much profit is expected to be made in that business going forward.

Jhunjhunwala said that he considers at the company's growth, valuation, liquidity, and cash flow. "I also take the loss of betting on the wrong company. If I buy shares of any company, I adopt that company. If it is not able to give a profit, then it is my wrong choice. It is true that some companies come to me for valuation. I choose the rest myself."

Some of his friends mention how if he (Jhunjhunwala) believed in something, then would he put his trust and money in it. For example, he held substantial shares of 'Bata' and 'McDowell's' as he saw an opportunity in them; but he sold those shares without making enormous profits. He says that time has taught him not to be stubborn. 'The habit of not being obstinate has taught me how to make better bets.' His friend Kalpraj Dharmasi says of him, that he always took the contrary decisions, as opportunities lie there.

❑

Share Marketing Tips

The following are some key tips to earn money based on Jhunjhunwala shares:

Don't Invest Based on Others' Decisions

One should not invest money in a stock just because others are investing in it; others may have the ability to take on losses, but not you. Investing in the stock market is not always as safe as banks. The stock market may give big returns, but the risk is big too. Therefore, it is important that you invest money only after getting complete information about the company.

Look at the Cash Surplus

Dividends play a pivotal role in the stock market. If the company has been paying regular dividends for a long time, it means that it is not short of cash. Companies with cash surpluses often do well. If the company performs well in the stock market, it is not necessary that it will give you exceptional returns. Therefore, it is important to do a background check of the company before investing and see how much dividend the company has given.

Don't Invest all your Money at Once

There is nothing wrong with a desire to make profits, but the rule says that only a small investment guarantees better returns. You may have a substantial amount to invest, but it is not necessary that you invest all the money at once. While investing money in any one stock, divide your investment amount into various portions and buy from time to time. If the stock goes down, keep buying. This will reduce the average of your purchases.

Investing in the stock market is not always as safe as banks. The stock market may give big returns, but the risk is big too. Therefore, it is important that you invest money only after getting complete information about the company.

Give Time to your Investments

According to Jhunjhunwala, it is better that one gives time for money to mature in the market. One may have to wait for a while, but the return will be guaranteed. Rakesh Jhunjhunwala's approach has always been to invest in the long term. He often advises beginners to invest for a long time. He believes that instead of earning profits in the short term, the investment should be given more time to grow manifold.

Don't Look at the Price of the Stock But the Value of the Company

Often people prefer to buy the higher priced shares, but it is important to see how the company has performed in the last one to five years. If the company has a bright and positive outlook, it will give you good returns despite the ups and downs in the stock market. Rakesh Jhunjhunwala says that the share price of the company should not determine whether you should invest in it or not; rather, the value of the company matters more. That is, before investing in a company, analyse that company very well. While investing in the stock market, looking at only one or two things does not work. One must undertake multiple analyses and has to understand well the management of the company.

According to Jhunjhunwala, it is better that one gives time for money to mature in the market. One may have to wait for a while, but the return will be guaranteed.

Look at the Company's Debt

Make sure to review the company's debt before investing. In the stock market, it is necessary to see how much debt the companies have; if the debt is less then the company will not have the pressure of availability of cash, but if the debt is high then the valuation of the company may fluctuate at any time.

Don't Worry about Committing or Making a Mistake

If you are afraid of making a mistake, then you will never be able to take the right decision. So, if you want to be successful, you will need to make decisions in life. Sometimes mistakes happen while making decisions. You learn from those mistakes. They can take you a long way. According to Jhunjhunwala, the best way to learn to invest in the stock market is through experience and through mistakes. One must make many decisions while investing in the stock market, and hence one is likely to make mistakes. So, learn from your own mistakes before blaming others.

If you are afraid of making a mistake, then you will never be able to take the right decision. So, if you want to be successful, you will need to make decisions in life.

Market is Supreme

Rakesh Jhunjhunwala believed that the market is supreme. The market is never right or wrong, it is us that are right or wrong. If you don't accept your mistakes and don't take lessons from them, you will never be able to become an astute investor.

Keep your Trading and Investment Portfolio Separate

If you are investing in the stock market for the first time and want to trade, then keep your investment and trading portfolio separate. Before trading each time, consider what the worst-case scenario could be. Be prepared for that scenario. Take only as much risk as you can afford.

The Right Way to Make Investments

Avoid investing in the stock market on the advice of a big stock buyer or on the advice of someone else. This is not the right way to invest. If you like or prefer any stock, then definitely analyse it yourself.

If you are investing in the stock market for the first time and want to trade, then keep your investment and trading portfolio separate.

Pay Attention to these Five Features

Private equity investors must look at five features before investing in the stock of any company. The five characteristics of the company can make their shares a multi-bagger. These five characteristics are patience, technology, frugality, method of management and governance. Indigo and D-Mart have scaled new heights in the last ten years or decade on the strength of these five features. If there is no patience in the company, then this is the biggest mistake in doing business.

Better Opportunities to Invest in the Shares

It is a good opportunity and it is advisable to invest in PSU (public sector undertaking) stocks, as the public sector companies will be the biggest winners after the corporate tax deduction. If the government's divestment plan is implemented properly, then PSU Companies will benefit tremendously. It will be worthwhile to invest in both Equity and Gold for the next 5 years. Gold may rise to $ 2,500 to $ 3,000 per troy ounce.

Companies that are Struggling Can Make You Rich

Each company can be classified separately, but it is not important to consider which company will survive and which will grow indiscriminately. What is important is the price of the company's share. Some of the best returns can come from companies that will now find it difficult to survive.

Summary

- In times of recession, more attention should be paid to the portfolio.
- Don't be in a hurry to sell the stock at a low profit.
- Check your portfolio at least twice a day.
- Invest money only when you get the right opportunity and keep your focus on returns.
- Have faith and confidence in yourself while investing.
- More important than investing is the return you will get from it.
- Don't overlook small stocks.

❑

Rakesh Jhunjhunwala's Portfolio

From Rs. 5000 to Rs. 44,300 crores! According to the latest update of 'Forbes', Rakesh Jhunjhunwala's net worth was $ 5.8 billion, which is equal to more than Rs. 44,300 crores. So how did a common man from Mumbai became one of the most successful stock investors in Indian history with only Rs. 5,000?

Rakesh Jhunjhunwala managed a privately owned stock trading firm named 'Rare Enterprises'. The name was derived from the first two initials of his and his wife's name Mrs. Rekha Jhunjhunwala.

During his long and eventful career in the stock market, Rakesh Jhunjhunwala had invested in many multi-bagger stocks.

In 2002-03, Rakesh Jhunjhunwala bought Titan Company Limited at an average price of Rs. 3, and recently it was trading at a price of Rs. 2,160. He held more than 42 million shares of Titan Company. His overall holding in the company as of June 2021 was 4.8 per cent.

Rakesh Jhunjhunwala managed a privately owned stock trading firm named 'Rare Enterprises'. The name was derived from the first two initials of his and his wife's name Mrs. Rekha Jhunjhunwala.

In the year 2006, he invested in Lupin and his average purchase price was Rs. 150. Recently, Lupin was trading at Rs. 951.

Some of the other multi-baggers in Rakesh Jhunjhunwala's portfolio were 'CRISIL', 'Praj India', 'Aurobindo Pharma', 'NCC', etc.

In previous years, Rakesh Jhunjhunwala once again made headlines for earning Rs. 50 crore in just 8 days.

Rakesh Jhunjhunwala was also a film producer apart from being on the Board of Directors of major companies like Prime Focus Limited, Geojit BNP Paribas Financial Services, Praj Industries, Concord Biotech, etc.

He has produced films like *English Vinglish*, *Shamitabh*, *Ki & Ka*. He is the Chairman of Hungama Digital Media Entertainment Pvt. Ltd.

Rakesh Jhunjhunwala's Latest Stock Portfolio

Here are the latest stocks with the highest weightage in Rakesh Jhunjhunwala's portfolio (updated as of December 2021):

S.NO.	Name of the Company	Quarter	No. of Shares	Present Value	%	Total Value
1.	Canara Bank	Sept-21	2,90,97,400	202.1	1.6	Rs. 6,17,73,78,020
2.	Wockhardt Limited	Sept-21	25,00,005	414.2	2.26	Rs. 1,06,75,02,135
3.	Orient Cement Limited	Sept-21	25,00,000	159.95	1.22	Rs. 40,88,75,000
4.	National Aluminium Company Limited	Sept-21	2,50,00,000	98.7	1.36	Rs. 2,52,00,00,000
5.	NCC Limited	Sept-21	7,83,33,266	70.45	12.84	Rs. 5,66,34,95,131.80
6.	Agro Tech Foods Limited	Sept-21	20,03,259	960.1	8.22	Rs. 1,91,61,17,233.50
7.	Tata Communications Limited	Sept-21	30,75,687	1354.2	1.08	Rs. 4,21,92,27,426.60
8.	Fortis Healthcare Limited	Sept-21	3,19,50,000	276.3	4.23	Rs. 9,26,23,05,000
9.	Aptech Limited	Sept-21	1,81,12,312	356.85	44.43	Rs. 6,69,06,88,052.80
10.	Indian Hotels Company Limited	Sept-21	2,50,10,000	190.9	2.1	Rs. 4,87,69,50,000

Rakesh Jhunjhunwala: Stock Market Philosophy

Rakesh Jhunjhunwala considered himself to be both a trader and a long-term investor. He observed: "Short-term trading is for short term profit. Long-term trading is for long-term capital formation. Trading is what gives you capital to invest. My trading also helps my investments in the sense that I often use extensive technical analysis for trading (which is then helpful for the investments).

Passionate investors always make money in the stock markets. If you work with passion, then you will never fail in any venture.

If the stock is high, I should sell. But my trading skills tell me that the stock may remain overvalued or fetch higher values. So, I stick to my investment.

So, I think they (trading and investing) complement each other in many ways; But they are two different compartments altogether."

> ***Rakesh Jhunjhunwala was also a film producer apart from being on the Board of Directors of major companies like Prime Focus Limited, Geojit BNP Paribas Financial Services, Praj Industries, Concord Biotech, etc.***

Rakesh Jhunjhunwala was extremely optimistic about India's growing economy and its success as an emerging market. Overall, his success story is really inspiring for investors, both new and old.

Rakesh Jhunjhunwala was a bear or a bull?

> ***Passionate investors always make money in the stock markets. If you work with passion, then you will never fail in any venture.***

Rakesh Jhunjhunwala, also known as the 'Big Bull' in India, was extremely bullish on the long-term growth of the Indian economy and the Indian equity market. However, he was once a bear during the days of Harshad Mehta and made a lot of money by shorting shares after the Harshad Mehta scam in 1992. At that time, he was part of the bear cartel along with other bears like Manu Manek and R.K. Damani.

What was Jhunjhunwala buying?

In the quarter of September 2021, Rakesh Jhunjhunwala entered three new stocks — Nalco, Canara Bank, and Indiabulls Real Estate. Before this, Steel Authority of India Limited (SAIL) was another new company in which the 'Big Bull' Rakesh Jhunjhunwala bought a fresh stake in the April-June 2021 quarter. Apart from this, Rakesh Jhunjhunwala had invested in Akasa Air recently to enter the airline industry.

His December quarter's holding details will be coming out soon. In this quarter, he kept his holding in Federal Bank, his preferred bank stock, at the same level as in the previous quarter. He had bought stakes in Federal Bank in the September quarter. If we look at the performance of Federal Bank's stock, it has gained more than 28 percent in the last one year. Rakesh Jhunjhunwala and Associates recently had 37 stocks in its portfolio.

Jhunjhunwala's Investment in Federal Bank

Rakesh Jhunjhunwala and Associates owns 3.7 per cent (7,57,21,060 shares) in Federal Bank, according to the company's shareholding pattern information published on the BSE's website for the December quarter. This investment in Federal Bank is in the personal capacity of Rakesh Jhunjhunwala and his wife Rekha Jhunjhunwala. According to the data, Rakesh Jhunjhunwala's holding in Federal Bank is 2.64 per cent (5,47,21,060) and Rakesh Jhunjhunwala and Rekha Jhunjhunwala's joint holding is 1.01 per cent (2,10,00,000) in the December 2021 quarter. Jhunjhunwala's holding in Federal Bank was valued at Rs. 730.3 crore as of January 12, 2022.

Jhunjhunwala, also known as the 'Big Bull' in India, was extremely bullish on the long-term growth of the Indian economy and the Indian equity market.

Federal Bank: Share Price Increased by 28 per cent in One Year

If one looks at the performance of the private sector Federal Bank in the last one year, the stock has gained more than 28 percent so far. The growth of the stock in the last 5 years has exceeded 35 per cent. The Federal Bank share price stood at Rs. 98 in the trading session on January 12, 2022.

Belief in Canara Bank too

Rakesh Jhunjhunwala held 1.6 per cent stake in Canara Bank. He included this stock in his portfolio only in the September quarter when he bought 1.6 per cent stake in the bank. This stake remained intact in the December quarter as well. He held a total of 2,90,97,400 shares of the bank, which were recently valued at Rs. 648.9 crores. Canara Bank has given 61 per cent returns to investors in the last 1 year.

According to the data, Rakesh Jhunjhunwala's holding in Federal Bank is 2.64 per cent (5,47,21,060) and Rakesh Jhunjhunwala and Rekha Jhunjhunwala's joint holding is 1.01 per cent (2,10,00,000) in the December 2021 quarter.

Federal Bank, which was included in Rakesh Jhunjhunwala's portfolio, provides for an immense earning opportunity. Because of its outstanding fundamentals, brokerage houses have been bullish on Big Bull's favourite stock. Apart from this, all the brokerage houses have been positive about the stock of this bank and have also increased the target. According to the brokerage house, Federal Bank is in a strong position amongst the mid-tier private banking sector. Its asset quality has continuously improved.

According to the report, Federal Bank has a stronger position in the mid-tier private banking sector. The bank's capital also appears to be in superb shape. It has an excellent network and given the focus on digital (economy) is increasing, it is also a favourable sign. The focus of the bank has increased on high margin business such as retail products, commercial vehicle loans, construction equipment loans, micro credit, and credit cards. The ratio has improved. There is strength at the management level as well.

According to the report, Federal Bank has a stronger position in the mid-tier private banking sector. The bank's capital also appears to be in superb shape.

Shares held by Rakesh Jhunjhunwala

After showing strong numbers, this stock held by Rakesh Jhunjhunwala, indicates an upward move. At the same time, according to stock market experts, Federal Bank has shown strong business momentum and its shares can see an appreciable jump in the coming times. Federal Bank's advances increased by 3.4 per cent to Rs. 1,37,3091 crores on a quarterly basis, indicating strong business momentum.

Deposits increased by 2.5 per cent on a quarterly basis to Rs. 1,68,743 crores, according to the report, whereas the CASA Ratio improved by 135 bps to 36.16 per cent in the same quarter. At present, an improvement in business momentum and a decline in asset quality and credit cost for Federal Bank is expected.

Rakesh Jhunjhunwala's Stake

Rakesh Jhunjhunwala held 3.7 per cent stake in Federal Bank. He had increased his stake by 0.9 per cent in the September quarter and before his held 7,57,21,060 shares of the company worth Rs. 768.9 crores.

According to stock market experts, Federal Bank has shown strong business momentum and its shares can see an appreciable jump in the coming times.

37 Stakes in his Portfolio

The veteran investor Rakesh Jhunjhunwala had reduced his portfolio from 39 to 37 stocks in last few years. In the December quarter, he sold his stake in Torque Ltd. and the Mandhana Retail Ventures. The net worth of these 37 stocks of the Jhunjhunwala's Portfolio was more than Rs. 25,538.7 crores as on January 12, 2022. Investors in the stock market kept an eye on Jhunjhunwala's portfolio.

Rakesh Jhunjhunwala's Wife

Rakesh Jhunjhunwala married Rekha Jhunjhunwala in February 1987. He has a daughter and twin sons.

Rekha Jhunjhunwala is also the co-owner of Rare Enterprises, a privately owned stock trading firm of Rakesh Jhunjhunwala.

Rakesh Jhunjhunwala's Airline

The Rakesh Jhunjhunwala-backed airline is known as 'Akasa Air'. He was the co-founder of this latest airline and owned 40 per cent of the company along with Aditya Ghosh, former IndiGo chairman, who holds a 10 perc cent stake in Akasa Air. The airline started operations in the summer of 2022 and is planning ultra-low-cost domestic flights.

Rakesh Jhunjhunwala's first successful investment was in Tata Tea in 1986, in which he bought 5,000 shares for Rs. 43, which later increased to Rs. 143 in three months, giving him more than three times returns.

Rakesh Jhunjhunwala's Fame

Rakesh Jhunjhunwala's first successful investment was in Tata Tea in 1986, in which he bought 5,000 shares for Rs. 43, which later increased to Rs. 143 in three months, giving him more than three times returns. His other successful investments in future include Tata Power, Sesa Goa (now Vedanta Ltd.), Praj Industries Ltd., etc. which made him famous in the Indian stock market.

What did Rakesh Jhunjhunwala say about Harshad Mehta?

Rakesh Jhunjhunwala said that the valuation of the market during Harshad Mehta's time was unbelievable. However, he also admitted in an interview that Harshad Mehta would have gone bankrupt if he had kept scamming for one more month.

Mogul of Dalal Street

Jhunjhunwala was a risk taker from the beginning. He borrowed money from his brother's customers and promised to return it with returns higher than the bank's fixed deposits. He made his first big profit in 1986, when he bought 5,000 shares of Tata Tea for Rs. 43 and within three months the stock rose to Rs. 143. He made more than three times profit. He earned Rs. 20 to 25 lakhs in a year.

Jhunjhunwala was a risk taker from the beginning. He borrowed money from his brother's customers and promised to return it with returns higher than the bank's fixed deposits.

Rakesh Jhunjhunwala was the 36th richest person in India, with a net worth of $ 5.8 billion.

Philanthropy

Mr. Jhunjhunwala was also a philanthropist and affirmed that the ultimate provider is God. He gave us a duty to use this money for altruistic social purposes. So, it is the purpose and ambition of my life that a sizeable part of my earnings is used for worthwhile social purposes. The only fixed income I have is dividend income and I spend one-third of my dividend income on charity, and I hope to continue doing so in the future.

Rakesh Jhunjhunwala was fond of food and enjoyed Chinese cuisine the most. He also liked watching cooking shows.

His philanthropic portfolio included nutrition and education and he contributed to a shelter for children with cancer run by St. Jude's. He supported Agastya International Foundation and Arpan — an organization that helps create awareness about sexual abuse among children. He also supported Ashoka University, the Friends of Tribals Society, and the Olympic Gold Quest. He was in the process of building an eye hospital in Navi Mumbai, which will conduct 15,000 eye surgeries free of cost.

Gastronome

Rakesh Jhunjhunwala was fond of food and enjoyed Chinese cuisine the most. He also liked watching cooking shows.

Controversy

In 2020, SEBI investigated for alleged insider trading in shares of the IT based education firm APTECH owned by him and his family. The board sent a 'show cause' notice and said that it was going to freeze Jhunjhunwala's bank accounts. The Investigating Officers probed the time between February 2016 and September 2016, during which he had made the alleged profit.

Favourite

Food	: Dosas
Dish	: Sugar
Actors	: Amitabh Bachchan, Aamir Khan
Actress	: Waheeda Rahman
Filmmaker	: Guru Dutt

Shares of Rakesh Jhunjhunwala

Rakesh Jhunjhunwala was often referred to as the Warren Buffet of India. He was one of the most successful investors in India and began investing with Rs. 5,000 in 1985, when the BSE index was at 150. Making the right decisions, investing in potential multi-baggers, and adapting the portfolio as per the requirement are some of the key priorities for Rakesh while investing.

As per information available on the stock exchanges, Rakesh Jhunjhunwala held these shares. As some companies may file their quarterly results later, these results are not available for such companies.

1. Agro Tech Foods Limited
2. Anant Raj Limited
3. Aptech Limited
4. Bilcare Limited
5. Crisil Limited
6. DB Realty Limited
7. Delta Corp Limited
8. Edelweiss Financial Services Limited
9. Escorts Limited
10. Firstsource Solutions Limited
11. Fortis Healthcare Limited
12. Geojit Financial Services Limited
13. GMR Infrastructure Limited
14. Ion Exchange (India) Limited
15. Jubilant Pharmova Limited
16. Karur Vysya Limited
17. Lupin Limited
18. Man Infraconstruction Limited
19. Multi Commodity Exchange of India Limited
20. NCC Limited
21. Orient Cement Limited

22. Prakash Industries Limited
23. Prakash Pipes Limited
24. Prozone Intu Properties Limited
25. Rallis India Limited
26. Federal Bank Limited
27. Mandhana Retail Venture Limited
28. Titan Company Limited
29. TV18 Broadcast Limited
30. VIP Industries Limited
31. Auto Line Industries Limited
32. Dishman Carbogen Amcis Limited
33. Indian Hotels Company Limited
34. Tata Motors Limited
35. VA Tech Wabag Limited
36. Indiabulls Real Estate Limited
37. TARC Limited
38. Tata Communications Limited
39. Tata Motors Limited — DVR ordinary
40. Wockhardt Limited
41. Jubilant Ingrevia Limited
42. Nazara Technologies Limited

43. Indiabulls Housing Finance Limited
44. Steel Authority of India Limited
45. Canara Bank
46. National Aluminium Company Limited
47. Metro Brands Limited
48. Star Health and Allied Insurance Limited

❑

Rakesh Jhunjhunwala: Perspective

Rakesh Jhunjhunwala asked his father to enter the world of the stock market after completing his studies as a Chartered Accountant. At that time, his father flatly refused to give the money as he knew that the stock market was not a child's play. Hence, he did not give money to Rakesh to enter this world. It is believed that later his father asked him to borrow or accept money from his friends and invest in the stock market. In this manner, some time elapsed but Rakesh remained adamant on his insistence to enter the world of the stock market. Eventually the year 1985 arrived and that is when he entered the stock market. Rakesh Jhunjhunwala entered into the stock market in the year 1985 by depositing his hard-earned money of Rs. 5,000 and after some time he saw a favourable opportunity to earn money in the stock market.

In the coming few years, Rakesh made outstanding profits from many stocks. During the years 1986-89 he earned a profit of more than 20 lakhs from his experience. Rakesh invested an enormous amount in the stock market with the expectation of a boom and his guess turned out to be correct. After the budget, the market gained momentum and Rakesh Jhunjhunwala's net worth rose from Rs. 2 crore straight to Rs. 40 to 50 crores. His outlook was extremely positive, for example:

- Often people prefer higher priced shares. But it is important to see how the company has performed in the last one to five years.
- If you are afraid of making a mistake, then you will never be able to make the right or appropriate decision.
- If you have made up your mind to earn money, then it is not necessary to start with a sizeable amount. You can become rich even from small beginnings.
- If a company gives dividends on a regular basis, it means that there is no shortage of cash with that company.
- Not having patience is the biggest mistake in doing business.
- If the stock goes down or declines, then continue buying. This will reduce the average of your purchases.
- Don't forget your roots.
- Stay simple.
- You can learn everything from your mistakes.
- Don't follow people, but instead people should follow you.

- Your stance should be bullish. Most of the gains in the market come from maintaining the bullish trend.
- An investor should always be like a chameleon. They should believe in themselves and stick to that investment by making the right investment at the right time.
- The price of a company's stock does not determine whether you should invest in it or not; rather, the value of the company matters more.
- While investing money in any one share, divide your investment into multiple amounts and buy from time to time or periodically.
- Divide the total amount into multiple amounts and buy incrementally.
- Learn from mistakes. They can take you a long way.
- Whether someone is watching or not, stay obsessed with your every move.
- Instead of making profits in a short period of time, the investment should be given time to multiply.
- Small investments make big funds; but one can get returns only with the right strategy and investing money correctly in the stock market.
- One's purpose in life should be to do what we love and enjoy what we do.
- Don't be greedy or avaricious for high returns. Invest if you are looking for 15 to 20 per cent returns.

- Trading always keeps you on your feet. It keeps you alert.
- Trading is fast paced. It works on the principles of quick give and take and kill and run. Everyone wants to make money from trading, but it is not possible. I have lost money too.
- We make mistakes every day in trading.
- Abuse of the system is part of every market.
- Everyone dominates in the boom, and everyone falls in the recession.
- Learn from your own mistakes before blaming others.
- Before investing, check for companies with less debt.
- Passion is essential for a successful investment.
- Markets reflect economic reality and fundamentals.
- The market is never right or wrong. It is us who are right or wrong.
- The market works. It is the best system to build a society.
- Allow the money in the market to mature. You will have to wait for a while, but the return will definitely be available.
- Either you don't enter the market or don't regret your actions.
- Making any reform in India is not easy.

- Every time is the right time to invest in the market.
- I feel anxious, curious, and eager to know about the market which is quite common.
- The desire to make profits is good, but the rule says that incremental investment alone can guarantee better returns.
- I have no clients other than my wife because I do not want to be accountable to anyone.
- I follow the law word for word. If the government has the right to check everything, we will have to accept it whether we like it or not. And this is part of life.
- I am not running a relay race. Nor am I in a rat race with anyone. I don't want to be richer than anyone nor do I want to be the richest man.
- I am obsessed. I don't know if I'm a philosopher or not, but I am definitely observant.
- I am fearless. I don't care what people think. I am only concerned about my actions.
- I don't want to go to a market to be famous. I want to go there to earn money.
- I hold investments for a long period because time has taught me that one should be greedy for a long time. So, when you have something promising, stick to it.
- I am doing what I enjoy doing.

- Don't try to be who you are not.
- Decisions in trading and investing are very lonely or solitary decisions and I can certainly do business without talking to anyone.
- If the company performs well in the stock market, then it is not necessary that it will give you handsome returns.
- Investing in the stock market is not always as safe as investing in banks. Here there is a big return but so is the risk. That is why it is important that you invest money only after obtaining complete information about the company.
- If you want to be successful, then you will have to make decisions in life.
- You make the biggest mistakes in the best of times.
- Don't pretend to be civilised.
- Buy the right stock at the right time and hold on to it.
- The best way to learn investing in the stock market is through experience; and experience comes from mistakes.

❑

Investment in Akasa Air

Rakesh Jhunjhunwala, also known as the 'Warren Buffet of India' for his successful stock investments, partnered with former IndiGo executives Aditya Ghosh and Vinay Dube, to meet the demand for domestic air travel. Consequently, SNV Aviation Private Limited is entering the Indian Aviation Sector with the brand name 'Akasa Air.' The Ministry of Civil Aviation granted a 'No Objection Certificate' (NOC) for Akasa Air's operations in India on October 11, 2021.

Rakesh Jhunjhunwala-backed Akasa Air started its first commercial operation on August 7, 2022, between Mumbai and Ahmedabad. Managing Director, CEO and Co-Founder of Akasa Air, Vinay Dube, said that Akasa is not an ultra-low-cost carrier, but a low-cost carrier, that is, it is a cheap airline.

After acquiring the 'No Objection Certificate' (NOC) from the Ministry of Civil Aviation, the company applied for AOP. SNV Aviation Private Limited entered the Indian Aviation Sector with the brand name 'Akasa Air.'

Akasa flights do not have ovens for hot food. The passengers need to keep the packed Upma/Noodles/Poha/ Biryani in hot water for a few minutes before eating. The airline has a few surprises for comfortable travel, which put Akasa ahead of anyone else in its category. The recruitment process of personnel like Pilots, Cabin Crew and Airport Staff for Akasa was completed way before it started operating.

Rakesh Jhunjhunwala, also known as the 'Warren Buffet of India' for his successful stock investments, partnered with former IndiGo executives Aditya Ghosh and Vinay Dube, to meet the demand for domestic air travel.

According to Dube, they wanted to be an affordable airline and that is their business model. They have the same type of aircraft, the same class of seats, no business class, and a premium economy. They also have buy-on-board like other (airlines) in their category.

Akasa received its first Boeing 737 MAX aircraft on the morning of June 21, 2022, and its first commercial flight took place on August 7, 2022. Akasa will have 18 aircraft by the end of March 2023. It will then annually add 12-14 MAX aircraft over the next four years, taking its fleet (order) to 72 aircraft. The Akasa Air brand will have 20 aircraft by the summer of this year. It will then immediately apply for the rights to fly overseas if it meets the 0/20 rule (i.e., no age limit, but a minimum fleet of 20 aircraft). Once permitted, it will start flying to places like Gulf, SAARC, and Southeast Asia.

As Akasa Air is a low-cost airline, it does not offer free Wi-Fi service. The airline's head office is in Mumbai, even though Akasa airline was in talks with various airport operators to decide on the primary hub based on the availability of check-in counters, parking slots and office space.

Akasa received its first Boeing 737 MAX aircraft on the morning of June 21, 2022, and its first commercial flight took place on August 7, 2022. Akasa will have 18 aircraft by the end of March 2023.

Akasa Air does not fly metro-to-metro cities but focuses on metro-to-tier-2 cities. Currently, it serves fourteen destinations with plans to launch three more destinations. In such a situation, it is difficult to say which city is its focus city. It still needs to develop an understanding of slots, parking ways, and check-in counters and this is still going on. Akasa said that they loved to serve Mumbai, as it is their home and headquarters, and also it is a prominent part of their network.

Founding Team of Akasa Air

Vinay Dube : Founder, Managing Director, and Chief Executive Officer

Aditya Ghosh : Co-Founder

Praveen B. Iyer : Co-Founder and Chief Commercial Officer

Belson Coutinho : Co-Founder and Chief Marketing Officer

Anand Srinivasan : Co-Founder and Chief Information Officer

Bhavin Joshi : Co-Founder and SVP of leasing and procurement

Neelu Khatri : Co-Founder and SVP of Corporate Affairs

Sanjay Dube : Co-Founder

Niraj Dube : Co-Founder

Akasa-affiliated Dube is a former CEO of Jet Airways, while Aditya Ghosh, who spent a decade with IndiGo, is credited for IndiGo's early success.

Akasa Air's vision is to be the most trusted and dependable airline in India with values below 8.

Branding

On December 22, 2021, Akasa Air unveiled its 'brand logo' and identity based on 'The Rising a Theme'. Elements of Akasa inspire its people. It symbolises the following three things:

- Sun's heat
- A bird's smooth flight
- Reliability of an aircraft wing.

The brand's tagline is 'It's Your Sky', which evokes the feeling of an inclusive brand experience that Akasa embraces everyone.

India's billionaire businessman Rakesh Jhunjhunwala had invested $ 35 million for a 40 per cent stake in Carrier.

Fleet

On November 16, 2021, Akasa Air placed an order for 72 Boeing-737 MAX aircraft, valued at approximately $ 9 billion. The order includes the 737 MAX 8 and the higher-end 737 MAX 200 variants.

❑

Disinvestment Must Come Back on Track: Jhunjhunwala

Question: The disinvestment of Air India is a momentous decision in the aviation sector. Tata has bought it and disinvestment is on track, so what does this mean for the market?

Jhunjhunwala: This time it is on track. I think BPCL, LIC, Container Corporation, and Shipping Corporation — I understand that from now till March 31, 2022, there are going to be 8-10 significant disinvestments. In this, LIC will also be involved. LIC (disinvestment) wouldn't be strategic. I think the government is very serious on this subject and there is great interest in the bidders as well.

Question: When you met the Prime Minister, many things happened. The pictures went viral. Why is a stockbroker meeting the prime minister?

Jhunjhunwala: Let me make one thing very clear — I pay $ 15 lakh million in brokerage every year, so I am not a broker. I pay $ 15 lakh million in brokerage. I am not a broker and why did the Prime Minister meet me — that you should ask him. I don't know why he met me!

Question: Many years ago, you said that democracy is the biggest obstacle to progress in India. Your statement had drawn numerous comments.

Jhunjhunwala: I would never have said such a thing. If you look back at history, the societies which have achieved and maintained prosperity, have two qualities — skills and democracy. In life, I have always said this, and democracy creates busyness. It gives people the power to think. It gives mentally developed people the power to act. If someone gives me $ 20 million, I won't teach my children in Singapore, but I would like them to ask—why? Tennis courts and swimming pools are not necessary. It is important to develop the minds of our children. From day one, they should be rebels, this is democracy. And the second thing is a skill. That is why I think our democracy has deep roots. For 20 years, i.e., from 1989 to 2014, there were coalition governments in the country, and I can tell you one thing that the right to information is a law and I would appreciate the press people, even if they do not agree on many things. However, our press is free. That is why I would have never said that democracy is most important. See, what happens is that when a man is hungry and naked, he does not have food to eat, then there is no difference between democracy and dictatorship for him. Don't you see what is happening in China? If his stomach is full, he eats meat, if per capita is 15 thousand dollars, then he wants freedom. We do not know what kind of social turmoil will arise in China and one of the reasons why they do not want it to subside is that they do not want social disturbance. They know that as soon as the pace of development slows down, there will be social turmoil. You look at Korea, you look at Taiwan, there was a dictatorship till the time they became prosperous, but that must be maintained. Look, India has inherent assets. Of the entire GDP of the world in the year 1640, 35 per cent of it was ours and when the British left it was 2 per cent. Today it is 7 per cent. So, I am bullish, and I am bullish on the stock market as well.

You are aware that in 2008, the share of the corporate GDP was 8 per cent. In 2019-20, it was 3 per cent. Corporate as a share of GDP in the US is at 11 per cent.

Question: Right now, we are at 16,000 so what is the target? Do you think India will be on par with China in the next 15 years?

Jhunjhunwala: Look, when I lie down after drinking 4-5 pegs, I know that Rekha is going to get angry. I do not know how angry she is going to be. We can know the direction; we cannot know the quantity or quantum.

Question: At least tell us something. Like in the next year or the next two years?

Jhunjhunwala: I don't know. Look, one day the Sensex will be at 5 lakhs, but I don't know after how many years that day will come. But I am bullish. We are in a position where India has never reached economically. We live in a country with a trillion dollars in savings. It is as true as much I am bullish about the land that if I take the land, I will go there on Sunday, on Monday and will see the land. It is better that I buy it directly from DLF. So, when the market is facilitating, then why will people not invest?

❑

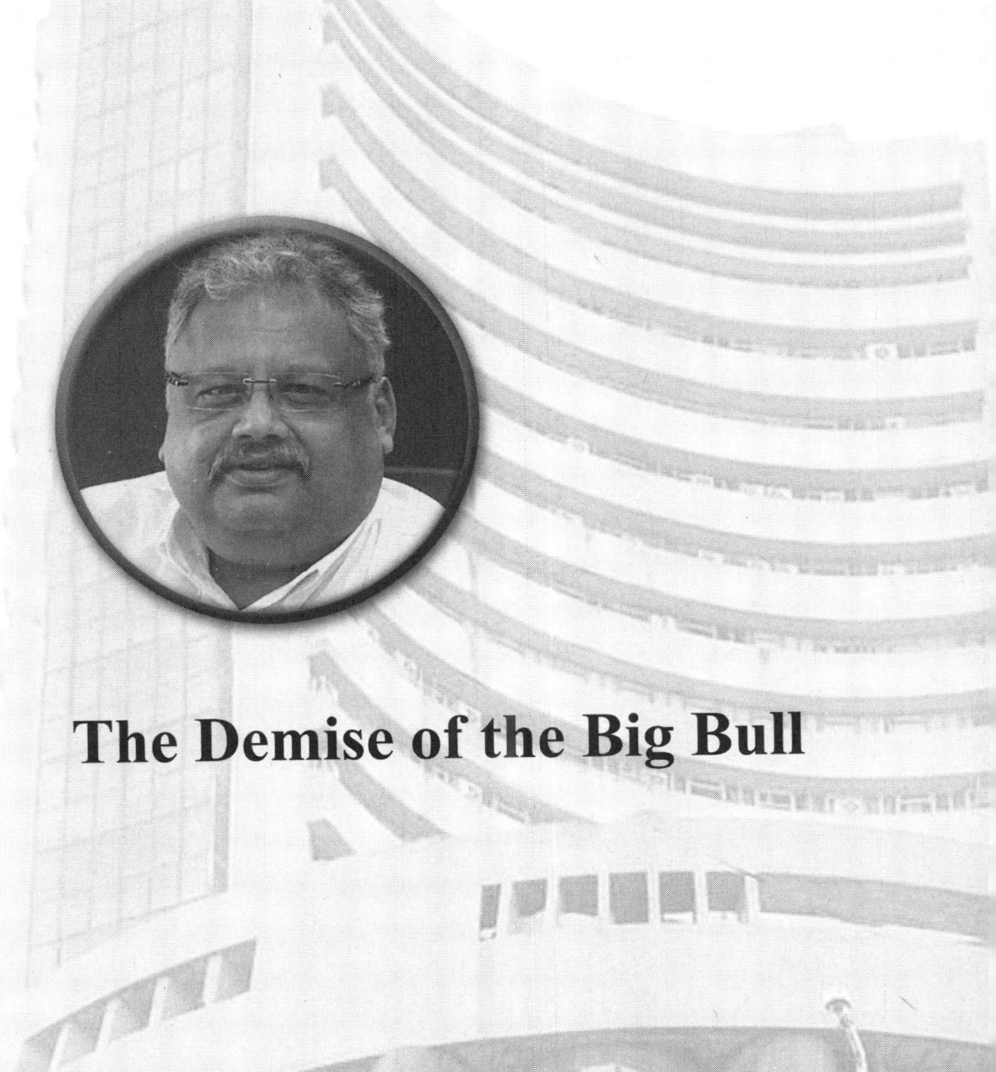

The Demise of the Big Bull

On August 14, 2022, India lost its "Big Bull" and master stock-market investor, Rakesh Jhunjhunwala. At the age of sixty-two, he breathes his last breath at Breach Candy Hospital, Mumbai. He was rushed to the hospital after he suffered a cardiac arrest. Later, the hospital authorities announced his demise. The Big Bull survived through his wife Rekha Jhunjhunwala and their three children.

Rakesh Jhunjhunwala got his nickname the "Big Bull" due to his bullish outlook on India's growth. In the opinion of Arun Kejriwal, founder of Kejriwal Research, "He was a speculator, an investor, and an entrepreneur, who knew how to play on fear and greed of people." He added, "The one important lesson that he has taught the market is that no matter how big your position is, you need to call it quits when the market goes against you."

Before he passed away, Rakesh Jhunjhunwala spent the last few weeks in and out of Breach Candy Hospital because reportedly both of his Kidneys have failed. Thus, he was going through dialysis regularly. According to his close friends and kin, he had not been doing well for the last two years due to diabetes and health issues related to the kidneys and acute organ failure. Often, he was on a wheelchair or bed rest.

Expressing his grief on India's Warren Buffett's demise, Prime Minister, Narender Modi tweeted, "Rakesh Jhunjhunwala was indomitable. Full of life, witty and insightful, he leaves behind an indelible contribution to the financial world. He was also deeply passionate about India's progress. His passing away is saddening. My condolences to his family and admirers. Om Shanti."

In December 2021, Rakesh Jhunjhunwala made his last public appearance at the launch of India's cheapest airline, Akasa Air. He was one of the co-founders of the airline. During the event, it was clear to all that he was not doing well as he looked frail sitting in a wheelchair.

The Akasa Air also commented on Big Bull's demise, saying, "We are deeply saddened by the untimely demise of Mr Rakesh Jhunjhunwala this morning. Our thoughts and prayers are with Mr Jhunjhunwala's family and friends. May his soul rest in peace." They further said, "We at Akasa cannot thank Mr Jhunjhunwala enough for being an early believer in us and putting his trust and faith in us to build a world-class airline. Mr Jhunjhunwala had an invincible spirit, was deeply passionate about everything Indian and cared greatly for the well-being of our employees and customers. Akasa Air will honour Mr Jhunjhunwala's legacy, values, and belief in us by striving to run a great airline."

According to the Forbes list of 2021, Rakesh Jhunjhunwala was India's 36th wealthiest person. As reported by the sources, his net worth at the time of his demise was $ 5.80 billion (Rs. 44300 crores) and he was considered the 438th richest person in the world by Forbes. He served as an inspiration and role model to all young investors.

Stocks from organisations like Star Health, Nazara Technologies, Tata Motors, IHCL, Agro Tech Foods, Canara Bank, Escorts, Rallis India, and Titan are among Jhunjhunwala's inventory. He served on the boards of several organisations, including Aptech, in which he owned a sizable interest. Additionally, he had invested in several startups.

India's Warren Buffett will always be remembered by us, and he will continue to live between us through his essential teachings and works.

❑

Interview-1

Rakesh Jhunjhunwala was an Indian businessman. He was known as the 'Big Bull' or 'Phoenix' of the Indian stock market. He started his journey with a capital of only Rs. 5,000 and built an empire of about Rs. 44,300 crores. Rakesh developed an interest in the stock market very early after listening to his father discuss various stocks with his friends. Here is a long interview with him.

Question: It is 9 in the morning, and we are outside the Bombay Stock Exchange (BSE). Do you feel emotional when you walk on this road? This is where you started your career about 35 years ago.

Rakesh Jhunjhunwala: I can tell you that I started here in 1985. I know many people here. I had no office here; I used to come here with my bag, and we used to get tickets to enter the ring. I did not get permission, so I used to stand outside the ring and watch the trading happen and that is how I learned. I remember how I struggled and raised money.

It is a very happy moment. There was a *samosawala* here. We used to eat *samosas* in the same garden.

Once there was a bomb explosion in BSE. I was inside the ring on the day of the explosion. Two samosa sellers were killed here. We had 12 exits from the ring. There was tremendous panic after the bomb blast. I was terrified of the stampede and kept shouting, "Don't worry, if we die, we will die together. Don't try to protect just yourself." And I saw a scene in the gallery ring. The glass broke and one person's head was cut in the ring. I have very vivid and sad memories of that day. But this street really reminds me of how I used to come here.

I can tell you that I started here in 1985. I know many people here. I had no office here; I used to come here with my bag, and we used to get tickets to enter the ring

Question: Everyone saw how the Mumbai Stock Exchange was back on its feet so quickly after the blast. Is there something about making money or trading that is tied to this 'never give up' attitude of the existence of the stock market?

Rakesh Jhunjhunwala: You know, trading always makes you stand on your feet. It keeps you alert. That is one reason I love doing business.

Question: What are the perspectives on life that you have learnt from your profession?

Rakesh Jhunjhunwala: The first thing I learnt is that the market works and it is the best system for building society.

Question: You are philosophical about what you do, aren't you?

Rakesh Jhunjhunwala: I am passionate. I do not know if I am a philosopher or not. I am definitely alert.

You know, trading always makes you stand on your feet. It keeps you alert. That is one reason I love doing business.

Question: The story of 'India Shining' — are you the face of that story, Rakesh Jhunjhunwala?

Rakesh Jhunjhunwala: Well, that is not what I meant to say. I entered when the market index was at 150. Today the index is at 12,000. That is eighty times. You know, I could have gone abroad too. I am a qualified Chartered Accountant. I could have started my practice. It is a fact that a person who started in the stock markets in India in 1985 can meet with success. This speaks volumes about the opportunities available here.

Question: Every step you take today, every investment you make, and every stock you put your money on, is tracked. There are people who jump on the bandwagon, whether you like it or not. Does it put pressure on you?

Rakesh Jhunjhunwala: Look, I do not have any clients other than my wife, because I don't want to be accountable to anyone. But there, I don't have a choice.

Question: Does this performance put pressure on you? For example, if a cricketer or soccer player starts performing well then there is always an expectation that whenever they go to the batting field, they will score 100 runs.

Rakesh Jhunjhunwala: Whether one is watching or not, I am always obsessed with my every move. The probability of my actions being successful gets better with experience. It will be better than what it was let us say five or ten years ago. The more (experience) the better. I am fearless and I do not care what people think. I am only concerned about my actions.

> ***Look, I do not have any clients other than my wife, because I don't want to be accountable to anyone. But there, I don't have a choice.***

Question: When someone is successful in the stock market, they become a role model. Are there too many Bunty Aur Bablis (those who want to take shortcuts) who want to be Rakesh? Do you think so?

Rakesh Jhunjhunwala: I get mails from many people who say that they want to invest in the markets and follow my career path. They want to know what I did.

Question: Ordinary investors, retirees. Do you think they want to get educated or do they just want to make quick money?

Rakesh Jhunjhunwala: Look, the market is for making money; but the market is also about knowledge. The market is also about ego. The market is also about the satisfaction of being proven right. Especially when that satisfaction comes from an original idea and not through a directed source or by following someone. That is why I feel anxiety, curiosity, and eagerness to know about the market. This is quite common, but in my opinion, the potential is quite limited because of the market being a market.

> ***I get mails from many people who say that they want to invest in the markets and follow my career path. They want to know what I did.***

Question: Greed and fear. You said that these are the two traits that one needs to balance. How does one balance them? Tell us an anecdote where you had to balance them.

Rakesh Jhunjhunwala: It is indeed so. Let's say, I invest in Titan. If I bought 'U' number shares, then I must have been very bullish, wouldn't I? And you would agree that if I put more than a certain percentage of my wealth into Titan, I would be greedy and demanding. I did not do it because of the fear that Titan may not do well, and I may lose even my principal amount.

Question: What about ACC? Did you really sell ACC for much less than before?

Rakesh Jhunjhunwala: It is said about the markets that either don't come to the markets or don't regret your actions. Isn't that, right? I think the results of the second quarter of 1991 would have been the best for ACC for the next 10 years. After those results came, I sold the shares. I bought them for Rs. 300 and sold them for Rs. 3,500. Within three months, the price rose to Rs. 10,000. But I have no regrets.

It is said about the markets that either don't come to the markets or don't regret your actions. Isn't that, right?

Question: You have no regrets; but which factor scared you at that time, fear or greed?

Rakesh Jhunjhunwala: I think I was neither greedy nor scared. I was just being rational.

Question: Celebrating the completion of three years of BSE's boom, the index has gone from 3,000 to over 12,000 in just three years and the investor believes that it will continue in the same way.

Rakesh Jhunjhunwala: You do know that the Sensex has gone from 3,000 to 12,000 in the last three years. You are aware that people are excited. Everyone is making money and hence the markets are making headlines. As they say, everyone parties in a boom and everyone falls into a recession.

Question: Whenever the market goes up, people get very excited and they also get very nervous, don't they? And you are the man they put forward to defend the bull run?

Rakesh Jhunjhunwala: There is no question of defending the bull run. Look, we forget what markets are. Markets reflect economic reality and fundamentals. I think India is heading towards unprecedented economic growth and the markets are just recognizing this.

Markets reflect economic reality and fundamentals. I think India is heading towards unprecedented economic growth and the markets are just recognizing this.

Question: Why is it so hard to believe what you are saying? Why do people have this fear psychosis that if things are good or favourable then they are bound to turn bad?

Rakesh Jhunjhunwala: I can think of two reasons, namely past experience and inertia of mind that people find it hard to believe that India can continue to grow economically. Also, in the past, we have had two scams in the stock market which made people very suspicious of the markets. Hence, I think there is a combination of reasons.

Question: Are you saying that we should not doubt the markets at this time?

Rakesh Jhunjhunwala: Well, I don't think there is any need to doubt. However, I think one needs to be cautious. I don't think there is any scam in the market.

One needs to understand one thing that the misuse of the system is a part of every market. We need to develop all markets. So, we need to reach that stage of development where people are taking advantage of the law.

Question: In the past, we have seen these two scams happen in the secondary markets and the primary market has been a safe haven for retail investors. Now it appears that even the primary markets look suspicious, right?

Rakesh Jhunjhunwala: One needs to understand one thing that the misuse of the system is a part of every market. We need to develop all markets. So, we need to reach that stage of development where people are taking advantage of the law. But the law will take hold, won't it?

Question: You have always defended the regulator by saying that the regulator exists and that the regulatory system and procedures are in place. Do you still believe that?

Rakesh Jhunjhunwala: Look, we can be critical of some of the mistakes made by the regulator; but we must realize that in Indian stock markets, we have become one of the most modern trading systems in the world and that too in a very short span of time. Every regulator has to evolve, and mistakes are going to happen during this development. So, I suppose it is a matter of a glass being half full or half empty.

Question: The irony is that Jhunjhunwala has all the elements of success, but he still sticks to his middle-class South Mumbai roots. How important is it to you for people to keep guessing how much you are worth?

I am not running a relay race and I am not in a rat race with anyone. Neither do I want to be richer than anyone, nor do I want to be the richest man. My purpose in life is to do what I love and enjoy what I do.

Rakesh Jhunjhunwala: What annoys me should not make any difference to others. Also, I am not running a relay race and I am not in a rat race with anyone. Neither do I want to be richer than anyone, nor do I want to be the richest man. My purpose in life is to do what I love and enjoy what I do. And money is a by-product of what I do. Why do people want to know what my wealth is? How is this relevant?

Question: Probably because your claim to fame is the money you have earned on your own? First-generation millionaire, who started at Rs. 5,000?

Rakesh Jhunjhunwala: I think what needs to be appreciated is not what I have, but how I made it. I am a wealthy person by the grace of God. How is it important, how rich I am? I can tell you one thing — I am rich enough that my wealth matters internationally.

Question: You just mentioned that you are not in the rat race. How do you react when you see these lists? World's 100 richest men, 100 richest Indians, 50 most powerful Indians? Because you are found in some of them, aren't you?

Essentially, decisions in trading and investing are very lonely and solitary decisions and I can certainly trade without talking to anyone. But I am used to talking to people.

Rakesh Jhunjhunwala: Well, I do not have a press agent and I do not have a press agency, and I am not seeking any publicity. But as long as a list is a recognition of human effort and human achievement, I would be lying if I said I do not like being on that list. So, I do like being there. But I am not making any special effort to be included in these lists. Being on these lists is a coincidence, not the purpose or objective of my work.

Question: So obviously there is no ambition to be on any other list and/or be higher up in some list?

Rakesh Jhunjhunwala: Not at all.

Question: You have often and firmly stressed that this business of yours involves extensive research, collecting considerable data and accumulating immense knowledge. What do you read?

Rakesh Jhunjhunwala: See, I read *The Economist* and *India Today* every week. In *The Economist*, I read the entire business section and the science and technology section. I read these constantly. Then I read the broker reports and look at the balance sheets.

Question: There are five screens here. Can you quickly tell us which of these does what?

Rakesh Jhunjhunwala: Well, these are live screens of BSE and. NSE where I track prices. These here are my investments. These here are the futures.

Question: There are 31 scripts here?

Rakesh Jhunjhunwala: Yes, except CL, these are all my investments. These are all the stocks in which I have some short-term positions. These are just some of the companies whose prices I want to follow, and these are the futures I trade. This is the live Reuters screen from where I get information. This is the internet and there is the television.

Question: If you want to, can you spend an entire day without talking to anyone outside?

Rakesh Jhunjhunwala: There are some people whose views I respect. There are some friends with whom I discuss matters, so I talk to them. Essentially, decisions in trading and investing are very lonely and solitary decisions and I can certainly trade without talking to anyone. But I am used to talking to people.

> ***I would not like to quote statistics. I merely make mistakes, which I can afford to amend, and I start again from there.***

Question: You know that I have spoken to some people who say that there is a contradiction in Rakesh. They say that he has been holding on to some shares for a really long time and here on his trading screen he can make and lose 20 to 50 crores in the blink of an eye. As we are talking, can you do that?

Rakesh Jhunjhunwala: Well, I don't do that kind of business. I keep investing for a long time, because I have read somewhere, and time has taught me that we should be greedy, but the greed should be long term. So, when you have something good, stick to it.

Question: What about the second screen?

Rakesh Jhunjhunwala: When I came to the market, I had no capital, nor father's gift and nor father-in-law's gift. So, I had to earn capital to invest. How do you invest if you do not have capital? I got all this capital by trading futures.

Question: And how much can you lose and how much can you earn?

Rakesh Jhunjhunwala: I would not like to quote statistics. I merely make mistakes, which I can afford to amend, and I start again from there.

Question: You come in even before the trends start to come in. For investment decisions?

Rakesh Jhunjhunwala: By the grace of God, I think from 1985-86 to 2006 I have been able to catch the most. Say, if there are 10 cycles in the market then I have been able to get 9 right. So, the cycle has been worthwhile and promising from an investment point of view. We make mistakes every day in trading. You know that one writer said that "it does not matter whether you are right or wrong in business. What matters is how much you lose when you are wrong and how much you earn when you are right."

We make mistakes every day in trading. You know that one writer said that "it does not matter whether you are right or wrong in business."

Question: If you lose money, do you feel stressed?

Rakesh Jhunjhunwala: No, never. I feel it for five minutes, because I am not investing more than 2 or 3 per cent of my wealth into it. I always remember Churchill's words.

Question: You just quoted Churchill. You quote regularly. Have you read anything else that these (non-investment legends) people have written?

Rakesh Jhunjhunwala: Well, Churchill was not an inspired investor.

Question: Exactly. So, do you read beyond the quotes you come across in books?

Rakesh Jhunjhunwala: I am greatly affected by the Second World War. I have seen a lot of movies on World War II. I watched 25 CDs on the Second World War and that gives you many quotes. Now my non-market, non-economic reading is very low. I was a voracious reader before 35.

> ***Where do I save my money? Well, the more I earn, the less my expenditure is, and more are my savings.***

Question: Even by international standards, it is your good wealth that you are selling. Does it mean that you are ready to trade and invest in international markets? What is stopping you? Is it because of legal issues or is it the scale?

Rakesh Jhunjhunwala: There are two to three reasons for this. First, even if I want to, I cannot-because all my wealth is in India. Second, the opportunity in India itself is so huge and so nascent. Why think about restaurants when we can have good food and delicacies at home? And third, I need to build a larger and more extensive organisation to invest internationally.

Question: In terms of capital, what do you need to invest to be considered a notable investor?

Rakesh Jhunjhunwala: I don't want to go to any market to be famous. I want to go there to earn money.

Question: So, capital is not a limit?

Rakesh Jhunjhunwala: No, capital is never a limit.

Question: You work with money. To put it simply, where do you save your money?

Rakesh Jhunjhunwala: Where do I save my money? Well, the more I earn, the less my expenditure is, and more are my savings.

I bought a painting last month. I have a house apart from this office, so no real estate either. I have invested in some real estate funds.

Question: Away from the stock markets, is there any area where you can save your money-art, real estate?

Rakesh Jhunjhunwala: No art. I bought a painting last month. I have a house apart from this office, so no real estate either. I have invested in some real estate funds.

Question: So, what are savings for Jhunjhunwala?

Rakesh Jhunjhunwala: My asset is a valuable portfolio. That is my saving.

Question: Could it be termed hypothetical — because depending on the markets it is up today and can go down tomorrow?

Rakesh Jhunjhunwala: I would not say that it is hypothetical, but it has its ups and downs.

Question: Doesn't it bother you sometimes that you are not the person with ideas? Instead, you are the person who is supporting others who have ideas.

Rakesh Jhunjhunwala: I do not think so. There are different parts to making anything. So, when I invest in a company at an early stage, I am working with that company. I would differentiate between my chairmanship of Aptech and my directorship of other companies. Due to such distinctions, we are running it properly.

> ***When I invest in a company at an early stage, I am working with that company. I would differentiate between my chairmanship of Aptech and my directorship of other companies. Due to such distinctions, we are running it properly.***

Question: How is the experience? This is a new experience for you, isn't it?

Rakesh Jhunjhunwala: It is a challenge and I don't know whether I will be successful or not. I will know in five years. But I like the challenge. Funds around the world have made billions of dollars by taking management control of companies. Now I had never taken management control of a company before Aptech. I think it will take 4 to 5 years.

Question: We talked about how the market is bullish all the time and when the Sensex keeps going up there is tremendous excitement and fear. Does it bother you that people like you are scrutinised too closely in such moments?

Rakesh Jhunjhunwala: I am concerned about one thing. I follow the law to the letter, and we live in a democracy. I work according to the laws of government institutions. Now if the government has the right to investigate everything, whether we like it or not, we must accept it and that is part of life.

Question: But this suspicion, which arises every time, especially in this business, does it bother you?

> ***Whatever I have done in life, people have looked at or viewed it with suspicion. Imagine that in the year 1985, a Chartered Accountant came from a bureaucratic family.***

Rakesh Jhunjhunwala: Not at all. Whatever I have done in life, people have looked at or viewed it with suspicion. Imagine that in the year 1985, a Chartered Accountant came from a bureaucratic family. He was going to the stock market and stood on these very streets. My father has been a member of the Wellington Club since 1973. I am a qualified Chartered Accountant. I do not think I did anything culturally wrong. But they do not want me to be a member of the Wellington Club. It is their choice. Initially, I used to react angrily to this. Now I react to it with maturity. People will have an opinion; time will change their opinion.

Question: If you have made your money as a trader or investor in the stock market then is it by no means equally respectable as the captains of the industry? Does that bother you? Because you are also putting in a huge amount of education and knowledge to make the kind of investment you are making?

Rakesh Jhunjhunwala: Let me tell you one thing and let me be very frank. For the kind of recognition I have received, I do not think honour is not there. If capitalism is the only form of government, then the temple of that form of government is the stock market. And trust me, I am not doing anything to be recognized by anyone. Recognition is accidental. I am doing what I enjoy doing.

> ***If capitalism is the only form of government, then the temple of that form of government is the stock market. And trust me, I am not doing anything to be recognized by anyone. Recognition is accidental. I am doing what I enjoy doing.***

Question: But Rakesh, you still remember the incident of not getting membership to the Wellington Club? Does this bother you a lot?

Rakesh Jhunjhunwala: But it was years ago when I may have felt a slight prick. Now I do not feel it. Jhunjhunwala prefers to live in a joint family. Without the financial and emotional support of his parents, he clearly would not have managed to throw a traditional or conventional career to the winds. Only his family members, including his sisters and brothers benefit from his stock tips. My father is the person who has taught me the most in life and I feel that he has a sizeable contribution in whatever I am in life. He is the most democratic father. I had a curiosity, and he has nurtured that curiosity.

Question: So, you are not a mother's boy, but a father's boy?

Rakesh Jhunjhunwala: No, I am the son of both my mother and father. I live with my parents, and we are a very close family.

I was very bullish on the market at that time as well and I had no reason to not be bullish. I feel the pace of correction is accelerating and, in the markets, I am as bullish as ever.

Question: We last spoke in June. That was the time when the pandemic was spreading in India. We were also in the middle of the harshest lockdown. You said then that you were getting somewhat disappointed. The development that has taken place, the reopening of the economy, the movement on the reforms front made by the government, are you less disappointed today, Rakesh Jhunjhunwala?

Rakesh Jhunjhunwala: No, I never said in June that I was disappointed. What I said at the time was that I was disappointed with the slow pace of reforms in India. I was very bullish on the market at that time as well and I had no reason to not be bullish. I feel the pace of correction is accelerating and, in the markets, I am as bullish as ever. I was very bullish in June and am still very bullish today.

Question: You were bullish on the markets in June as well, but you are right to say that you were disappointed with the pace of reforms. So, I want to ask you, now that we have seen more agricultural reforms, the way the government has responded to the Covid crisis, and the way we have announced labour reforms — how does India's story on the reform front appear to you today?

Rakesh Jhunjhunwala: We must remember one thing — it is not easy to undertake any reforms in India. Regarding the agricultural reforms — at least when I talk about the reforms with agriculture experts or agriculture companies, all of them are very excited about them. But look at the way the governments of Punjab, Haryana and Maharashtra are reacting. I personally feel that the government is undertaking excellent reforms and is prepared to undertake these reforms regardless of political opposition, whether from within or from the opposition. We have to look at things in a larger context. We are in a democracy, and we have to take people with us. I am very happy with the kind

We have to look at things in a larger context. We are in a democracy, and we have to take people with us. I am very happy with the kind of reforms the government is implementing and I think that next, they are going to pass the bill on electricity reforms in the parliament, which has already been prepared.

of reforms the government is implementing and I think that next, they are going to pass the bill on electricity reforms in the parliament, which has already been prepared. I consider this also a game-changer and I think this is going to be a strategic sale of Public Sector Undertakings (PSUs) only.

So, I am very happy now that we are picking up on the pace of reforms and we are trying to attract both foreign and Indian capital. We Indians should realise that it is not easy to reform and transform a democracy like India. Everything has a vested interest. So as compared to June, my frustration has abated by 80 per cent.

Ownership in India is now much lower than it was three years ago. So, there is going to be a tsunami of capital in both foreign and Indian stock markets; because most Indians and foreigners are still not enthusiastic about the Indian economy

Question: Given where the global economy finds itself with continued liberal monetary policies around the world, and increasing bond-buying programmes — what does all this mean in terms of liquidity and flows into India? When we spoke last time, you said how Foreign Institutional Investors' (FII) ownership in Nifty has halved in the last three years. What do you think it will look like going forward?

Rakesh Jhunjhunwala: I think money is coming neither slowly nor fast, but in a tsunami; because India is amongst the last frontiers of markets where substantial development can take place in the world. The world is full of fluidity. That liquidity has to find an outflow. Ownership in India is now much lower than it was three years ago. So, there is going to be a tsunami of capital in both foreign and Indian stock markets; because most Indians and foreigners are still not enthusiastic about the Indian economy and the signs of its recovery, but according to me, it is happening. Let's say you have 10 per cent negative growth this year. Next year we will have 10 per cent positive growth. I believe we are going to increase to 6-7-8-9 and 10. That's my opinion, I could be right or wrong — we will be at double-digit numbers in five years. There are uncertainties on our side, and I am optimistic for India more than anything else for the economic growth ahead.

> ***I believe that with lower interest rates and less exposure to Indian equities and a favourable outlook towards emerging markets in general and India in particular, the markets will be headed for a tsunami of money.***

Question: A clear claim in which you believe is that there is a tsunami of capital that will hit Indian markets and FDI; but what would it mean in the context of sectors? Which sectoral bets do you expect to make?

Rakesh Jhunjhunwala: It is a relay race and it is a buffet which everyone is going to attend. So, you believe in the Indian story and choose your stocks. I am sure that the Indian economy will grow. The fact is that corporate profits in India are at an all-time low relative to the Gross Domestic Product (GDP). In this case, there will be a double whammy. The percentage of profits in GDP will increase and the size of GDP will increase. Again, I believe that with lower interest rates and less exposure to Indian equities and a favourable outlook towards emerging markets in general and India in particular, the markets will be headed for a tsunami of money. I think India is where it was in 2003.

I see growth and prosperity coming. I could be wrong, and we are well on course to acquire equity, both locally and overseas. I think we are in a market that will surprise everyone.

Question: You talked about how India finds itself in a situation similar to where it was in 2003. What is your hypothesis there?

Rakesh Jhunjhunwala: My hypothesis is that India is going to the years of 2003-2009, (where) we are growing at 8-9 per cent. I think in the next four-five years we will be there. Secondly, there is probably disbelief in the markets. There is incredible power in the market. I think that at least for the next three-four years, there are going to be very low-interest rates worldwide. Several improvements are happening. Corporate profit is at an all-time low in GDP and I think GDP is going up. The ratio of corporate profits to GDP will increase. Indian companies are at the best potential they have ever been, and we have a clean system. Many rogue entrepreneurs have been fired. So, given all these factors, India is going to enter a period of very high growth. I see India differently from most Indians.

Metals, public sector, and other similar beaten-down stocks where there has been total mistrust in the market over the years. I think this is where the highest returns will come from.

I see growth and prosperity coming. I could be wrong, and we are well on course to acquire equity, both locally and overseas. I think we are in a market that will surprise everyone.

Question: Now I want to talk to you about pharma because the last time you said that pharma has scored 30-40 runs at that point in time and now it will hit a double century. It has been a rank outperformer, whether it is because of Covid, whether it is because of the China Plus One strategy, it is an area that has clearly seen a great deal of interest. Do you think there is more scope here?

Rakesh Jhunjhunwala: Last time I told you pharma has scored 30-40 runs, this time I will tell you that it is now at 40-42 runs.

Question: So, will you continue to bet here?

Rakesh Jhunjhunwala: Linear development is not going to happen in any area. After the rise, each sector is going to freeze for some time. Consolidate first and then take the next step. So, I am not smart enough to know that now the field has grown. It is going to consolidate for some time. So let me sell and buy another area. Then after three months, the second zone would peak, and then I should buy back. In the pharma sector, I am not smart enough to know when this will happen. I know it will go up. A period of consolidation and recovery is approaching, and I try not to time it so closely.

A fundamental change in the way the Government of India treats its assets better — not just to sell HPCL to IOC or sell REC to PFC but to do things in a more discreet way, which will create shareholder value and the first indicator of this is the buyback by HPCL.

Question: You had said that you believe this market is going to surprise us. Where do you think, this surprise is going to come from, I will try to link it with what you mentioned earlier. You said that some of the leading winners would be found in the most beaten-down areas. So where do you see this surprise coming from?

Rakesh Jhunjhunwala: In most of the beaten down stocks it could be metal or could be the public sector. Metals, public sector, and other similar beaten-down stocks where there has been total mistrust in the market over the years. I think this is where the highest returns will come from.

Question: Since you talked about the public sector, one of the things that you were expecting (to happen) is the topic of strategic disinvestment. In fact, I was talking to the Secretary of Economic Affairs, and he was very clear that there are obstacles. They accept that they (obstacles) are there for companies like BPCL, Container Corporation, etc.; but they still think they will move on. Do you believe that this is going to be a major topic that will be revisited this time?

> ***But the owner of these properties, mainly the Government of India, has now realised that we must work with governance and legitimate ways to increase the value of their assets.***

Rakesh Jhunjhunwala: No sir, see, there are two parts to the public sector. There is strategic disinvestment, but how do you handle the other valuations? These days you see HPCL, BPCL and so many stocks perhaps Cochin Shipyard — I don't want to name too many stocks and I don't have any of them. Maybe in HPCL, I have a small ownership. The question is whether you should be able to realise the value of strategic disinvestment. When will you realise the value? When the owner treats his share well. The buyback by HPCL is the first indicator that the Indian government now wants to be careful and wants to work to increase the valuation of its assets. This is a medium through which the value of public sector shares will increase. A fundamental change in the way the Government of India treats its assets better — not just to sell HPCL to IOC or sell REC to PFC but to do things in a more discreet way, which will create shareholder value and the first indicator of this is the buyback by HPCL. I do not think that it has happened without the knowledge and consent of the highest level of government. This is my guess.

This is one way that public sector stocks will gain value and second, certainly a strategic investment and third, asset monetization. I am told that they are promised that there will be no ETF. No sale other than strategic disinvestment and they will value that asset better and will not disinvest them randomly. I think this could lead to a massive revaluation of public sector stocks. So, the strategic sale is ultimate. But there are other factors that will lead to a better valuation.

Question: So, you expect a re-rating, if certainly this consistent strategy is concerned not only with strategic disinvestment but also with increasing shareholder value for public sector stocks?

Rakesh Jhunjhunwala: The first sign is buyback by HPCL and that is understandable. I think the buyback by HPCL means they are going to do it in many more companies — in various ways without any random disinvestment, by buybacks, in whatever way. But the owner of these properties, mainly the Government of India, has now realised that we must work with governance and legitimate ways to increase the value of their assets. The buyback in HPCL is important not only for HPCL, but it is important for what it indicates. But I am also not aware that whatever has happened is my estimate. Realising that there is considerable room for valuation in public sector stocks and this was not happening, as the government was doing it randomly. Now the government proposes to manage the assets better, as the buyback of HPCL indicates.

□

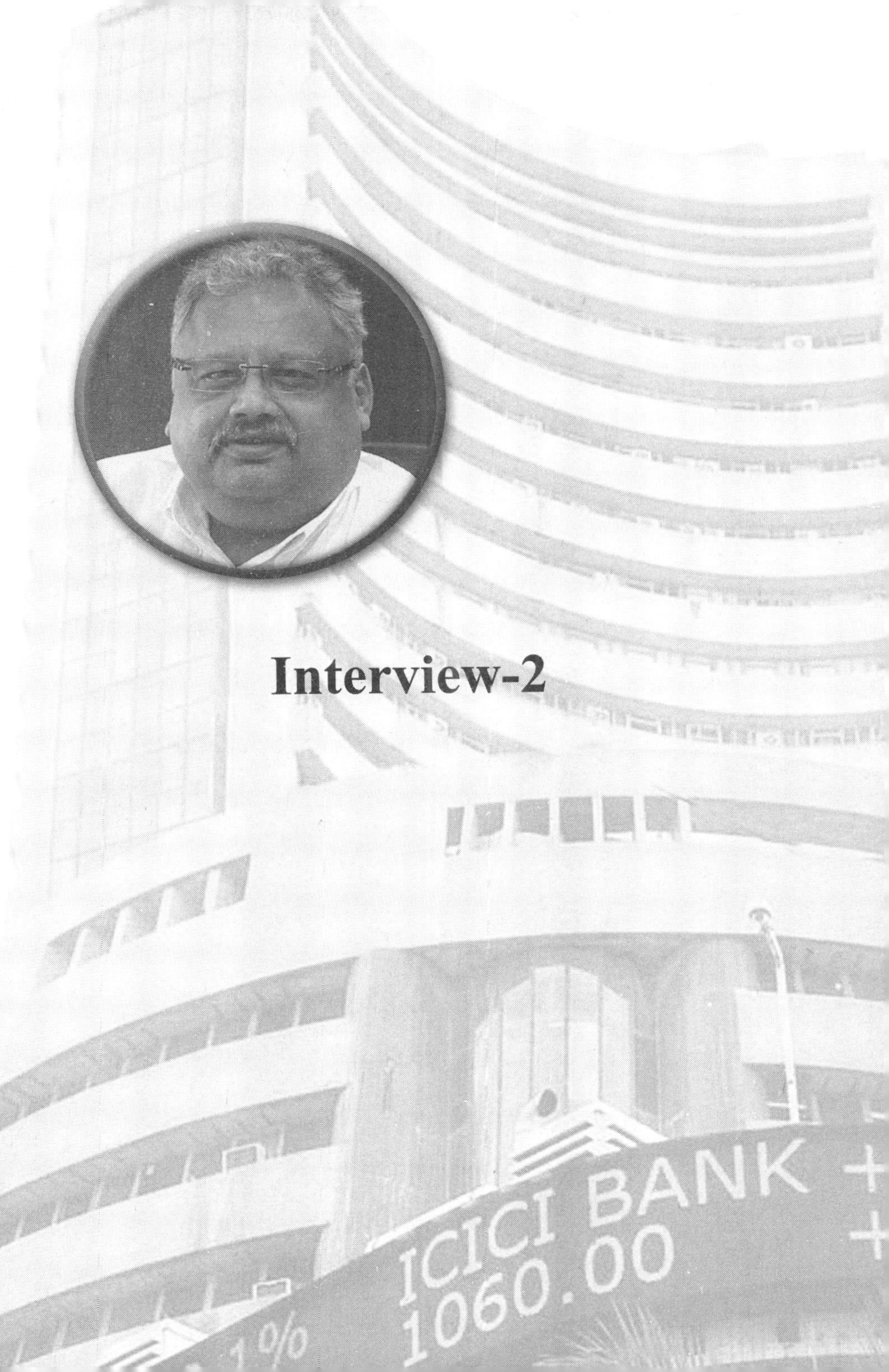

Interview-2

‘Big Bull’ of the Indian share market, Rakesh Jhunjhunwala, is an eminent Indian stock trader. Here is an exclusive conversation with him.

Question: Mr. Jhunjhunwala, first of all, I would like to know your opinion on the Union Budget. Do you think this Union Budget, in terms of its intent and purpose, will be able to accelerate the economy? As the Indian economy has come out of Covid with full force, will this budget be able to accelerate it?

Jhunjhunwala: Look, what Mr. Modi and his government is doing, is for long-term interests, not for short-term gains. And I think there are many far-reaching messages in this budget. First of all, I think that the ratio of tax to GDP and the amount of tax collected in this year’s budget will be much higher than expected. This indicates that the ratio of tax to GDP is increasing in India. Only when this happens, we will be able to spend more on social welfare and infrastructure. I think this is a very significant message. Then the other thing I think about is that do not give freebies beyond a limit. As the saying goes, if you give a fish to a person, he will eat it every day. If you teach him to fish, he will become self-sufficient. Therefore, according to me, development is the panacea for crores of people in India. Only development will increase jobs, increase social welfare and I was reading that the government is prepared to give a subsidy of 10 billion dollars to make chips (semi-conductor) in India. Therefore, there is a lot of thinking in the government at the strategic level, which is why development is the priority. This is the most important thing for the long-term benefit of all Indians, be they rich or poor. The second thing I see is that everyone is emphasising the jobs that are proposed to be created through investment in infrastructure. Government investment is important, but private sector investment is bigger than that. If you see anyone, be it Mr. Adani, Mr. Ambani, and Mr. Anil Agarwal, all want to invest in India. And one important fact that no one has mentioned. Everyone is talking about spending on infrastructure, but no one is talking about what will happen by investing in basic infrastructure. It will make the industries more competitive and efficient. We must not forget this. I think this is a very significant and crucial

Look, what Mr. Modi and his government is doing, is for long-term interests, not for short-term gains. And I think there are many far-reaching messages in this budget.

factor in capital expenditure on infrastructure. And it is a bold political statement, as the government has preferred development and fiscal prudence over populist measures. I feel whatever India is doing is a very big statement.

Question: Do you think there has been any major change in policymaking in India? The budget document is absolutely transparent, there is no change in tax when there could have been some changes in (Covid tax) taxes. Policymaking is more explicit and more stable in terms of supporting entrepreneurship.

Only development will increase jobs, increase social welfare and I was reading that the government is prepared to give a subsidy of 10 billion dollars to make chips (semi-conductor) in India.

Jhunjhunwala: Ultimately India will be built by entrepreneurs. Isn't that, right? The government has no reason to do business. I think Mr. Modi has said this in Parliament. And he wants to respect and encourage reasonable risk-taking. In my opinion, this country doesn't have capitalism or socialism, but what we have is realism. The amount of transparency the government is bringing in finance is very encouraging. Today we have the highest level of foreign exchange reserves, don't we? Our budget is absolutely transparent. Now there are no such elements to create imbalance. The FCI loan has been repaid. Air India's debt has been repaid. I am very optimistic about the fact that in this country, the level of GDP and the tax ratio will really reach unforeseen levels, and this will make government spending more appropriate and better.

Question: But are we taking a big risk at a time when the general level of inflation is high and if the supply constraints are not addressed from the budget and spending point of view, then could it lead to further inflation?

Ultimately India will be built by entrepreneurs. Isn't that, right? The government has no reason to do business. I think Mr. Modi has said this in Parliament.

Jhunjhunwala: I don't know whether it will increase inflation or not. Most of the inflation is commodity inflation and many of the commodities are linked to international prices. So, India's consumption of five per cent will not lead to a rise in the prices of commodities. India is still not such a major consumer of goods, that our consumption may cause prices to jump. The food inflation rate is not high at all. And 4-5 per cent inflation is expected.

Question: 4-6 per cent is the average inflation rate in India. So, are you anticipating an economy where the government has the problem of abundance or surplus? There is absolutely no manipulation of the corporate balance sheet. Except for the rural balance sheets, the retail balance sheet has also made a comeback. So, has it ever happened that India has been in such an appreciable position in terms of sales?

Jhunjhunwala: It is because of this reason that I say that the cycle of debt is now behind us. Capital expenditure is about to happen now. We have a vibrant corporate sector and we are 140 crore Indians. How can there be a shortage of food in a place where 2 lakh people are born every day? So, I am very optimistic and would also like to say that even though the budget figures are conventional, the Economic Survey has projected a real growth of 8 to 8.5 per cent. That is why I think that India is now dreaming of 10 per cent growth, and it is possible. Ease of doing business and change in the attitude of the government is what is more important. According to me, the PLI scheme will be an immense hit next year… I would also say that don't forget the 65 per cent of Indian Economic Services — Transport, trade, and hospitality, which have been the major contributors, and which suffered tremendously last year. So, the growth in these three sectors will be very high next year.

Capital expenditure is about to happen now. We have a vibrant corporate sector and we are 140 crore Indians. How can there be a shortage of food in a place where 2 lakh people are born every day?

Question: So, whether we believe it or not, we are still in a new credit cycle. We have moved on to the new capital cycle and are riding the earning cycle. So how will this credit cycle and earning cycle be different from the previous cycles?

Jhunjhunwala: I don't think it will be any different. There will be an increase in corporate profits every year the ratio of corporate profits to GDP is at 4 per cent. In the US it is 10 per cent. In 2008, we were at 8 per cent. That is why I suppose in the next five years we will be able to achieve GDP growth. If you reach 8 per cent of the GDP, then imagine that in 4-5 years if the GDP is at 5 lakh crores, then you know that the corporate profits will be unbelievably high — at 40 lakh crores.

There will be an increase in corporate profits every year the ratio of corporate profits to GDP is at 4 per cent. That is why I suppose in the next five years we will be able to achieve GDP growth.

Question: When I say that not the profit cycle but what about the sectors which will contribute because the previous credit cycle or earning cycle was driven by power, cement, and steel. So, will it be any different than that?

Jhunjhunwala: No, everyone will get a profit. I would say that I don't see much difference in this cycle for the IT sector. India is an exporter of IT and is a huge exporter. So, IT is eternal. I am very bullish on metals, infrastructure, and hospitality.

Question: Is there excessive fear domestically and abroad, about inflation?

Jhunjhunwala: Only time will tell. But some factors in the US are about to reverse and that is the prices of second-hand cars. Destruction in America will only last for a certain or specific period. In the USA, cheques are sent to people. When those cheques run out, people will have no choice but to go to work. Therefore, it is difficult to say that inflation will not increase more than expected. The fact is that Japan prints the most money in the world and there is no inflation in Japan. So, a low inflation rate is linked to population, isn't it? The population doesn't grow. And then there is technology, which reduces cost.

In the USA, cheques are sent to people. When those cheques run out, people will have no choice but to go to work. Therefore, it is difficult to say that inflation will not increase more than expected.

Question: We have seen and witnessed turmoil in the global equity market ever since the Fed changed its policies in December and early January. But the US stock market is quite mature. The ten-year paper has never gone above three or three and a half per cent in this kind of inflation. Why is that?

Jhunjhunwala: The reason is that the interest rate in the US is estimated to be 1.25 per cent. What is 1.25

per cent? And the stock market has risen with each cycle of rate hikes. So, I can't predict what will happen with the inflation rate, but I think the market is ready for inflation.

Question: One of your famous quotations is that the rate of interest acts like gravity. Now we can argue that it will increase three or four times, but we can definitely see that there are extraordinarily low-interest rates in India and globally. When will this law of gravity of higher interest rates start affecting the capitalist class?

Look, when the boom time comes and I don't know about the US, but as far as India is concerned, I don't think that an increase of 100-200 basis points in interest will have any impact on corporate investment.

Jhunjhunwala: Look, when the boom time comes and I don't know about the US, but as far as India is concerned, I don't think that an increase of 100-200 basis points in interest will have any impact on corporate investment. The impact will be on the consumption of households, as you cannot keep the interest rates at 6.8 per cent and home loan rates at 6.5 per cent. I don't think any other sector will be affected so negatively.

Question: Everyone was waiting for two things that happened at the beginning of the year. One was the Fed and the other was the budget. We have now moved past the risk of both. Now, what is the most significant thing on which the markets should keep a watch?

Jhunjhunwala: I think that will be the end of Covid. That is the biggest thing. And the continuation of disinvestment by the government.

Question: From the market's point of view, adjusting to Covid has now become history. Has the market gone beyond it?

Jhunjhunwala: No one can guess that. We only get two or three months when the world is without a new variant. Once it becomes like a common cold, that is when I think we will move ahead of it and that is when the government will allow normal business to happen because it would have become like a common cold by then. The only thing is that it (Covid) is very effective.

This question was based on train travel from Churchgate to Chandivali in Mumbai. If the market starts rallying, then it moves from Churchgate to Chandivali.

Question: I asked you this question in February last year. I would like to ask the same thing once again. This question was based on train travel from Churchgate to Chandivali in Mumbai. If the market starts rallying, then it moves from Churchgate to Chandivali. You told me in March last year that the market rally had only reached Charni Road. Has the bull market gone beyond that now?

Jhunjhunwala: Probably started from Charni Road and reached till Central.

Question: Well, so that means, there is still a long way to go?

Ultimately, earnings will have to remain a slave to the cash valuations. So, anyone can have their moment for some time, but it doesn't make much difference.

Jhunjhunwala: Yes.

Question: Will you be surprised if NIFTY goes below 15,000 in this bull market?

Jhunjhunwala: Anything can happen and if the NIFTY goes below 15,000, then it will not be a retreat of the bull market. But I think the probability of that happening is very low.

Question: The selling we have seen in global technology stocks is not actually selling but it was a stampede. So, what was due for a long time, is it over now?

Jhunjhunwala: It was not a stampede in global technology stocks but only that of inflated value stocks where dreams were being sold to people. I think it was a fairly good correction.

Question: Have the investors now understood that ultimately, buying is done by the companies with cash flows and that dreams cannot be bought?

Jhunjhunwala: What can we teach them whether they have understood or not? This has now become history. Ultimately, earnings will have to remain a slave to the cash valuations. So, anyone can have their moment for some time, but it doesn't make much difference.

Question: You anticipated a jump in two sectors, and you have frequently repeated them — Metals and PSU Banks. In the same context, you also gave a great example — how Shree Cement traded at a pre of 55,000 while Tata Steel was at 5,000. These should improve. Metals have made a decent comeback. Are you still anticipating a rise in the prices of metals?

I am everything in Tata Steel from a businessman to an investor. Take my words wisely. (About Air India) I am very happy.

Jhunjhunwala: Yes, I am.

Question: And if I were to ask why do you think so?

Jhunjhunwala: This year, the EBITA (earnings before interest, taxes, and amortization) of Tata Steel will be higher than that of the entire cement industry and its valuation will be 5 to 10 per cent of the cement industry. I think the highest level of margin of Indian operations is 30,000 and that a margin of 24-25 thousand per tonne will continue to sustain in the long run. And with their expansion, Tata Steel's base EBITA may be at 60,000 crores.

Question: As an investor, how excited are you about the privatisation of Air India?

Jhunjhunwala: I am everything in Tata Steel from a businessman to an investor. Take my words wisely. (About Air India) I am very happy. With due respect to Pandit Nehru, I would like to say that we bought it from the Tatas. We bore a loss of Rs. 1 lakh crore and sold it back to the Tatas. So, I don't understand what the use of all this was.

What were your thoughts when Titan went from 40 to 150? Titan had a minimum of Rs. 30, and it went to 150 and today I believe its effective price is 50,000.

Question: Can I say that this time, apart from tax collection, the government has kept a conservative estimate regarding the disinvestment target.

Jhunjhunwala: Given a great deal of uncertainty; they have done well with disinvestment. If it (disinvestment) becomes more than that, then that is good. I had a feeling that they would not undertake disinvestment, but after seeing the reactions and the interviews of all the bureaucrats and the finance minister, I think, they will actively undertake disinvestment. But they don't want to take credit for it unless there is a situation where they take the credit but nothing that they expected happens.

Question: PSU Banks have done very well. You said that this was a sector which had an average performance for over 10 years. And in 2020 you realise that there is great potential in this sector. Now the stock has risen. Has the re-rating been completed?

Jhunjhunwala: It has just started.

Question: Why are you saying this?

Jhunjhunwala: Because I think the prices will still go up a lot. What were your thoughts when Titan went from 40 to 150? Titan had a minimum of Rs. 30, and it went to 150 and today I believe its effective price is 50,000.

We were always trading at a premium. Even when Japan was at the bottom, it was still at a higher premium than the US. We always trade at a premium.

Question: There is a discussion among many global brokers that the Indian market is trading at a premium to other emerging markets.

Jhunjhunwala: Let them say that. Did they not sell 1 lakh 37 thousand crores and yet the market was stable? You are entitled to your opinion but you are not God. Did anything happen when you sold it?

Question: You have always said that domestic investors will return, and they have returned. Will they stay here? Will the asset allocation continue?

Jhunjhunwala: People say that 8 crore demat accounts have been opened, what will happen to the remaining 80 crores? India is expected to have savings of 2 to 2.5 billion dollars in the coming times. Where will this money go? It will become 2 to 2.5 trillion dollars.

Question: So, you are saying that this is simply a change in the allocation of assets by Indian investors?

Jhunjhunwala: Yes, first in financial assets and then in financial aid. Look, there are four ways to save. The first is real estate, jewellery, investing in your business or investing in financial assets. So, the percentage that is being invested in financial assets will accelerate. There will be an enormous increase in savings and the proportion of financial assets entering the stock market will also increase. So, it is going to grow tremendously.

I am very excited about the automobile sector and I think they will become the biggest players in electric vehicles locally and globally. Where in the world will you get an electric car for ten thousand dollars?

Question: The Indian market is currently trading at a premium. We are trading at a higher premium than other markets. Is it true?

Jhunjhunwala: We were always trading at a premium. Even when Japan was at the bottom, it was still at a higher premium than the US. We always trade at a premium.

Question: Will it remain at this level given that there are earnings, corporate governance, and policies of the government?

Jhunjhunwala: The day people will walk for the development of the Indian economy and when the corporate profit reaches 8 per cent of the GDP, they will contract.

Question: At the beginning of Covid, you had said that I am an extremely happy investor in the Tata Group of companies. And some of those companies have made remarkable comebacks, be it Tata Motors, Tata Consumers, or even Tata Communications. Are the depressed re-ratings for the Tata group companies behind them?

Jhunjhunwala: I cannot answer this question. Is it ahead or behind us? I am anticipating an appreciable bullishness on the prices. I still think there is a long road ahead of us.

Question: Tata is trying to do something very interesting, as they are leading the way through the EV chain through Tata Motors, Power, and Tata Chemicals. Are you excited about the EV space and what Tata is doing?

Jhunjhunwala: I am very excited about the automobile sector and I think they will become the biggest players in electric vehicles locally and globally. Where in the world will you get an electric car for ten thousand dollars?

Question: The last time we met, you had said that Tata Motors, in which you have invested, is on the cusp of a major transformation. Now which new company is on the cusp of such a change?

Jhunjhunwala: I am looking for it and will tell you when I find it.

Question: The rationale you gave for liking Tata group stocks is that you think that Chandra works according to cash flow, is technology savvy, understands skill and talks about size.

Jhunjhunwala: He is a sensible risk-taker. An aggressive but sensible risk-taker.

Question: So, your belief behind the Tata Group and Chandra is gone?

Jhunjhunwala: Absolutely.

So, you have seen the best times of the private banks. And where is the difference in valuation?

Question: You mentioned PSU banks, but private banks have not participated in the last one year. HDFC did not participate.

Jhunjhunwala: This is my point of view that in the next three years, the price and performance of the PSUs will leave the private sector banks far behind.

Question: But if the credit cycle starts, then private banks will also start giving corporate loans?

Jhunjhunwala: They will do corporate lending, but they had already been doing so. And their cost-to-income ratio is low. Their debts and their NPAs were less. So, you have seen the best times of the private banks. And where is the difference in valuation? After doubling, the market cap of Canara Bank is 45 thousand crores. Their book is as big as ICICI, so I am not saying that other banks will not do well. I think PSU Banks will perform better.

Question: Your three private companies have gone public in the last two years — Nazara, Metro, and Star. Where do you see more value as an investor—in the private sector or in the public sector?

Jhunjhunwala: My objective is that I have no rules. That is why we see the circumstances. Circumstances of different companies. We do not see that it is public, it is private.

Question: I will whip out a statement from last March. You said that you are very happy and if you are given 5 thousand crores then you can continue buying for a week. You can also give a subsidy of 5 thousand crores. Do you mean that there are sufficient opportunities in the market?

My objective is that I have no rules. That is why we see the circumstances. Circumstances of different companies. We do not see that it is public, it is private.

Jhunjhunwala: Yes, if I have money, I see a lot of opportunities.

Question: Can one assume that you can invest it carefully?

Jhunjhunwala: Yes, I can.

Question: Mr. Jhunjhunwala, there is a statement of yours which you often give on different platforms. The statement is, "I made money trading, but a normal investor shouldn't trade." The statement goes on, "Daddy told us not to drink whiskey but drank it himself."

Jhunjhunwala: There are age-old examples that out of 100 people who enter trading, 99 people lose money. But trading is so exciting, so people want to indulge in it.

Question: If you have to divide the market into two or three parts, as you have always done, then according to you, out of the market cap of India which is three trillion dollars, how much is overpriced? How much of it makes sense?

I have two investments, each worth a billion dollars. Titan is worth 1.75 billion, and I have invested in Star Health.

Jhunjhunwala: The Titan has been highly-priced throughout its life. If I had been guided by this theory of overpriced and underpriced, I would have sold Titan for 2500. Today it is 50,000.

Question: Why does this happen? Why do stocks maintain manifold premiums?

Jhunjhunwala: Because there is scope for growth in corporate governance. There is transparency, there is cash flow, and there is market leadership.

Question: There are two types of premium stocks; one — as you said, of those companies which are built on imagination and evaluation and second — of companies like Titan or Asian Paints or Pidilite. These are great companies, but they are expensive. What is the future of other companies that are reputable companies but don't have the right price multiple?

Jhunjhunwala: There can also be a correction in the price multiple. It is possible that two years' earnings may have been discounted, but what after that? I have sold Rs. 5 crore shares of Titan. And each time I have sold, the prices have risen.

Question: Let me go back slightly. In the year 2010. We were at an event in Oberoi where you said, "If Titan does not become a billion-dollar investment for me, I'll take that investment in the microwave." Would you like to add more names to this list?

The Titan has been highly-priced throughout its life. If I had been guided by this theory of overpriced and underpriced, I would have sold Titan for 2500. Today it is 50,000.

Jhunjhunwala: I don't know which names I can add. Maybe, I can talk about Star Health. I have two investments, each worth a billion dollars. Titan is worth 1.75 billion, and I have invested in Star Health.

Question: From the perspective of Covid, has the worst time for insurance and health insurance passed?

Jhunjhunwala: Let's hope so.

Question: This is an amazing sector sir — because the need for health insurance has increased, but the earnings have not increased accordingly.

Jhunjhunwala: But if the claim ratio does not come down, you will have to increase the premium.

Question: Are you sure that the insurance sector will come out of this?

Maybe, I can talk about Star Health. I have two investments, each worth a billion dollars. Titan is worth 1.75 billion, and I have invested in Star Health.

Jhunjhunwala: One big reason is Covid, the other is the phenomenal increase in hospital expenses. In the last two years, the inflation rate in hospitals has increased by 40 to 50 per cent and it is not likely to come down.

Question: But you have bought stocks in both Hospital and Healthcare. When I say healthcare, I mean Star Health. Can the two go hand in hand together as the loss of one may have to be compensated by the other?

Jhunjhunwala: No, it is not so. Both can be profitable.

Question: As an investor, are you somewhat disappointed about pharma as an investor?

Jhunjhunwala: I am not disappointed as I did not pick the right companies. So, I am disappointed with my decision. Why should I blame someone else?

Question: Time and again, something keeps going for the farmers. Sometimes the prices, sometimes the electricity, sometimes the US FDA — there is a plethora of problems. Two years ago, we thought that Pharma would go the IT way, but its curve has been quite different.

Jhunjhunwala: The US pharma market has not been doing well. Mainly because of Covid.

Question: Everyone is talking about the risk that may come from a meltdown of Crypto. Could this risk impact the (equity) asset class in this environment?

> ***I am not disappointed as I did not pick the right companies. So, I am disappointed with my decision. Why should I blame someone else?***

Jhunjhunwala: Maybe. But the equity investing class and the crypto investing class are completely different. I understand that one-day crypto will collapse. Where will they invest then?

Question: But you don't see the crypto meltdown impacting other assets? Isn't it big enough to backfire?

Jhunjhunwala: No, in general, it will not have any effect.

Question: Rakesh Jhunjhunwala makes decisions very quickly. Some of our common friends say that you decide to invest several million in 10 minutes. You don't spend hours; you do it in minutes. How does that work?

Jhunjhunwala: You have to understand the main points. Let me tell you that I do not want to be a victim of analysis paralysis. You are investing in a future that is uncertain. You cannot predict it beyond a certain limit.

Question: Some of our common friends say that Rakesh Jhunjhunwala has decided to reduce trading. Is that true?

Jhunjhunwala: What?

Question: They are saying that Rakesh Jhunjhunwala no longer wants to trade with the same aggression as before.

Jhunjhunwala: I have been feeling like this for the last 25 years about what to do, should I quit trading, but that leave is not there yet.

Question: Once a trader, forever a trader! Since you have invested in technology, I hope you are familiar with the meta-avatar that everyone is talking about, the meta world.

Jhunjhunwala: I don't know what it is.

Question: All right — Meta World has taken an avatar, so if Rakesh Jhunjhunwala had to take on a digital avatar, which avatar would you take?

Jhunjhunwala: I don't have any knowledge about it.

Question: Let us keep this question for next time. Last time you met you said I don't know what my daughter wants to do, what my eldest son wants to do, but my younger son is definitely interested in the market, and I am teaching him. How are you teaching him? What are you telling him?

Jhunjhunwala: Just adding briefly to his curiosity. But he is really interested.

Question: May I go over this broader notion about how things are as you mentioned? We are looking at India as it has never been before.

Jhunjhunwala: Absolutely. And people don't realise it. I wish every Indian felt that way. But don't try to make an atheist a believer, time will do that.

Question: For a SIP (SIP — Systematic Investment Plan) investor, is there a possibility and an expectation that there will be double-digit returns in the next 2-3 years?

Jhunjhunwala: Although it is difficult to estimate, the returns will be more than the expectation.

Question: I had kept the question of the bear market for the last. What are two or three factors that will satisfy you that this bull market is maturing or that the bull market has not progressed as you had thought or visualised it would? What are the factors that you would consider?

Jhunjhunwala: I think geopolitics is the biggest risk and whether Mr. Modi will continue as Prime Minister because now we know the kind of policies that are going to be made. There is stability now and a friendly attitude towards business. These are two important factors.

Question: Now I am tempted to ask one more small question and that is about the discussion among the general public that we saw a good 2021 where the index gave double-digit returns and 40-50 per cent for small and mid-cap indices. Do you expect this year to be a flat or inconsequential year with diminishing returns?

Jhunjhunwala: No, I do not think so. I think we will make a profit in this as well.

Question: This sounds like a headline. So, then what is going to happen this year according to you?

Jhunjhunwala: I can guess the direction, not the depth.

Question: Quantity? What do you think about that?

Jhunjhunwala: When I don't like to estimate it for myself, then how can I tell you?

Question: I respect that.

Jhunjhunwala: I don't think it will be a flat year. This will be a positive year.

Question: This will be a positive year. We are waiting for that. We appreciate that you took time out for us amidst the current volatility in the market. Thank you so much for giving us the time.

Jhunjhunwala: Thank you.

❑

Motivational Thoughts of Rakesh Jhunjhunwala

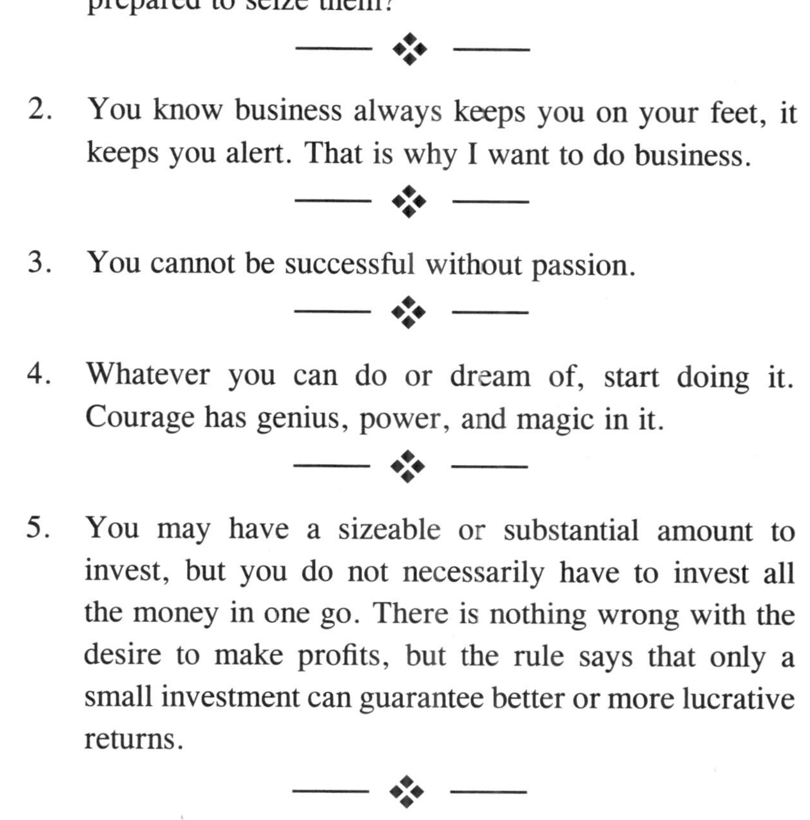

1. Opportunities will come and go, but are you ready or prepared to seize them?

—— ❖ ——

2. You know business always keeps you on your feet, it keeps you alert. That is why I want to do business.

—— ❖ ——

3. You cannot be successful without passion.

—— ❖ ——

4. Whatever you can do or dream of, start doing it. Courage has genius, power, and magic in it.

—— ❖ ——

5. You may have a sizeable or substantial amount to invest, but you do not necessarily have to invest all the money in one go. There is nothing wrong with the desire to make profits, but the rule says that only a small investment can guarantee better or more lucrative returns.

—— ❖ ——

6. You will never fail in anything if you do it with passion. Passionate investors always make money in the stock markets.

❖

7. Never waste your hard-earned money without proper research! Never invest according to stock tips.

❖

8. Invest in companies that have strong management and competitive advantage.

❖

9. Don't invest in cheap stocks that will give bountiful returns when your children grow up! Think about the appropriate timing too!

❖

10. Invest in a business, not a company.

❖

11. An investor should always know when and what they can lose.

❖

12. While investing money in any one share, divide your investment amount into smaller parts and keep buying from time to time or periodically. If the stock goes down then continue buying, this will reduce the average of your purchases.

❖

13. Invest in a business, not a company.

—— ❖ ——

14. Do not invest money in a stock just because others are investing in it; it is probable that others can bear losses, but you may not have that ability.

—— ❖ ——

15. Learn from mistakes, learn to take losses!

—— ❖ ——

16. Instead of making profits in the short term, the investment should be given time to grow manifold. Allow the money to mature in the market. You will have to wait for a while, but the return will be guaranteed.

—— ❖ ——

17. Invest in small caps, which will convert to large caps. The most ambitious challenge of investing is that you must understand whether the organisation has the potential to scale.

—— ❖ ——

18. When opportunities arise, they may come through technology, marketing, brands, value protection, capital, etc. You should be able to spot them.

—— ❖ ——

19. Invest when the stock is popular.

—— ❖ ——

20. Passionate investors always make a profit in the stock markets. If you, do it with passion, then you will never fail in anything.

21. Nobody can predict the weather, death, market and women.

22. Everyone makes a profit during the boom time, and everyone makes a loss during a slump.

23. Investing in stocks for a short period of time may yield some gains, but investing for a longer period will yield higher returns.

24. See the world as it is, rather than what you want it to be.

25. Never react or change your investment decisions according to daily business news.

26. The most important consideration while investing is for the investor to believe in themselves.

27. Be prepared to accept losses. They are part and parcel of the life of a market investor.

28. There are some similarities between wives and markets, you can argue with wives but not with markets.

29. Give your investment time to mature. Give the world time to find your gems.

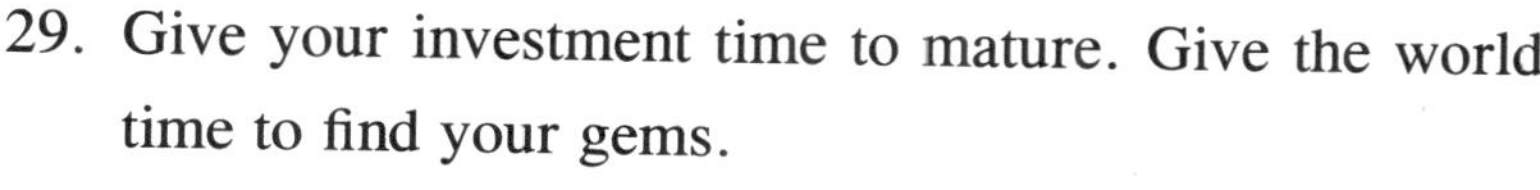

30. It is not wise to blindly follow the stock tips given by big investors.

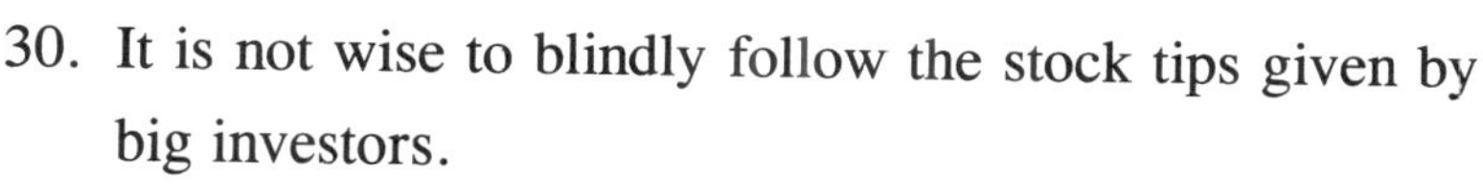

31. Keep an open mind and assess what is at stake. Also, be aware of when to take risks. You need to be responsible for it.

32. The market is like women, always commanding, mysterious, unpredictable, and volatile.

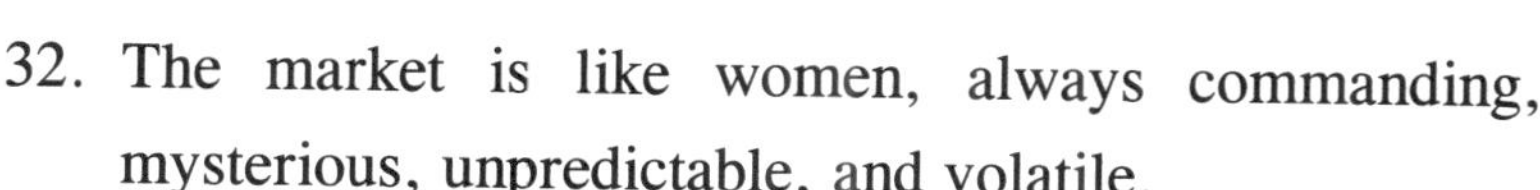

33. You must be like a chameleon in the market, always changing your colours and going with the trends. If you try to go against it, you will be lost.

34. The market is above individuals. The market is rational. A man can never be smarter than the market.

35. Never invest your hard-earned money in stocks without evaluating your investments and never invest according to various unreliable stock tips.

36. Increase profits and reduce losses.

37. I only make those mistakes which I can tolerate because I can pick myself up from there to start all over again.

38. I initially wanted to be a broker, but I did not have the capital to become a broker, so I started investing.

39. I am willing to take big risks that I can bear and then restart or resume all over again.

40. I have learned two things about women in general and wives — when they say something, don't react.

41. If you see an opportunity, grab or seize it immediately.

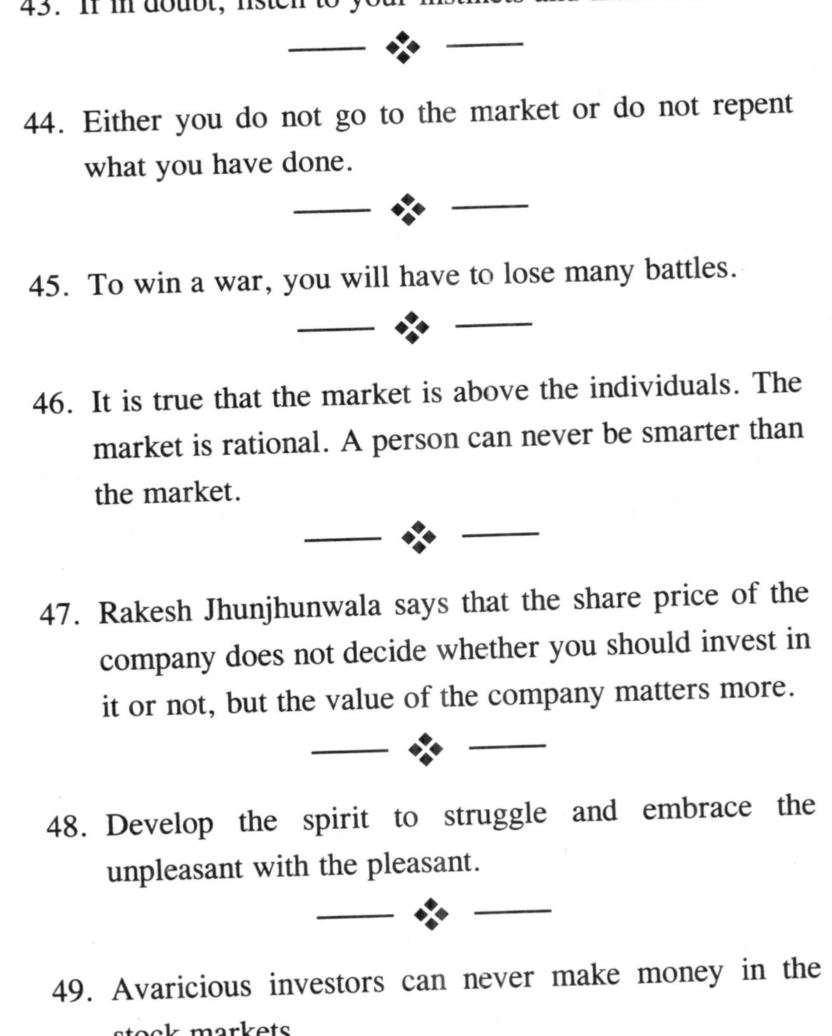

42. If you have any doubts, listen to your heart.

—— ❖ ——

43. If in doubt, listen to your instincts and intuition.

—— ❖ ——

44. Either you do not go to the market or do not repent what you have done.

—— ❖ ——

45. To win a war, you will have to lose many battles.

—— ❖ ——

46. It is true that the market is above the individuals. The market is rational. A person can never be smarter than the market.

—— ❖ ——

47. Rakesh Jhunjhunwala says that the share price of the company does not decide whether you should invest in it or not, but the value of the company matters more.

—— ❖ ——

48. Develop the spirit to struggle and embrace the unpleasant with the pleasant.

—— ❖ ——

49. Avaricious investors can never make money in the stock markets.

—— ❖ ——

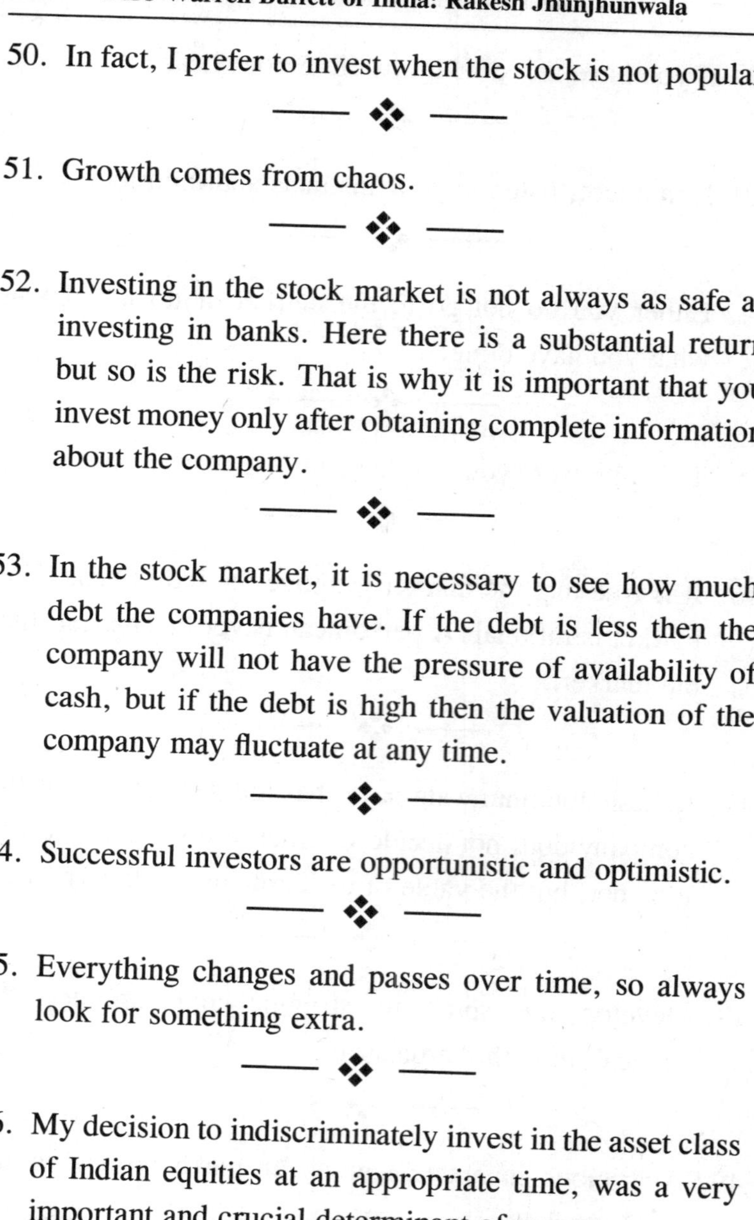

50. In fact, I prefer to invest when the stock is not popular.

51. Growth comes from chaos.

52. Investing in the stock market is not always as safe as investing in banks. Here there is a substantial return but so is the risk. That is why it is important that you invest money only after obtaining complete information about the company.

53. In the stock market, it is necessary to see how much debt the companies have. If the debt is less then the company will not have the pressure of availability of cash, but if the debt is high then the valuation of the company may fluctuate at any time.

54. Successful investors are opportunistic and optimistic.

55. Everything changes and passes over time, so always look for something extra.

56. My decision to indiscriminately invest in the asset class of Indian equities at an appropriate time, was a very important and crucial determinant of my success.

57. The best thing about a stock is that it must be cheap—the point of entry.

58. Always focus on what is at stake and when to take the risk.

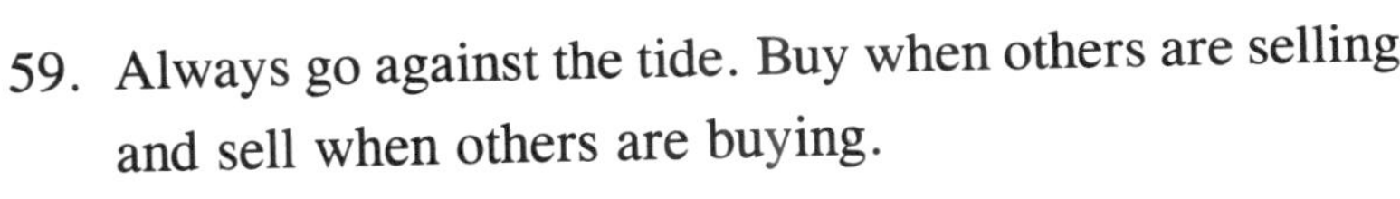

59. Always go against the tide. Buy when others are selling and sell when others are buying.

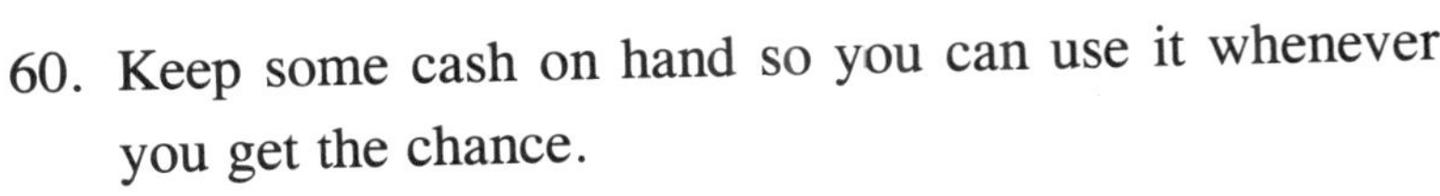

60. Keep some cash on hand so you can use it whenever you get the chance.

Padma Shri Awardee: Rakesh Jhunjhunwala

One of India's most pronounced civilian awards, the Padma Shri is given to people who have made significant contributions in various fields, including the arts, literature, social work, science and technology, medicine, sports, and others. It is the fourth-highest civilian award in India after the Bharat Ratna, Padma Vibhushan, and Padma Bhushan.

Over the years, many distinguished individuals have been conferred with the Padma Shri award, including artists, actors, social activists, scientists, and athletes. Renowned personalities such as Sachin Tendulkar, A.R. Rahman, Lata Mangeshkar, Satyajit Ray, Milkha Singh, and M.S. Subbulakshmi are some notable recipients of this award.

On March 22, 2023, the President of India, Droupadi Murmu, conferred the Padma awards on 106 renowned people. Among these 106 fortunate individuals, 6 people were honoured with Padma Vibhushan, 9 with Padma Bhushan, and 91 with Padma Shri award. Some prominent names included in this list are Zakir Hussain, Srinivas

Varadhan, Kumar Mangalam Birla, Mulayam Singh Yadav (Posthumously), and many others. Among these leading personalities comprised in this list, one name is Rakesh Jhunjhunwala.

Late master stock investor and the "Warren Buffett of India," Rakesh Jhunjhunwala, was honoured with Padma Shri (Posthumously) for his remarkable work in the field of trade and industry. His business partner and wife, Rekha Jhunjhunwala, received the Padma Shri on his behalf from President Droupadi Murmu during the investiture ceremony at the Rashtrapati Bhavan on Wednesday, March 22, 2023.

Rakesh Jhunjhunwala, the co-founder of India's cheapest airline, Akasa Air, passed away on August 14, 2022, after suffering from a cardiac arrest. He was born into a Rajasthani family in Mumbai. After graduating from Sydenham College in 1985, he enrolled at the Institute of Chartered Accountants of India. Later he married Rekha Jhunjhunwala, and they had three children—one daughter and two sons (twins).

Jhunjhunwala was famously known as the "Big Bull" because of his bullish attitude towards India's stock market and growth. It is said of Rakesh Jhunjhunwala that whichever stocks he purchased, generally turned to be multi-baggers stock. The legendary investor and business magnate, Rakesh Jhunjhunwala, will forever live in our memories.

❑❑❑